A History of the
BERRY SCHOOLS
—— *on the* ——
MOUNTAIN CAMPUS

Jennifer W. Dickey

A History of the

BERRY SCHOOLS

on the

MOUNTAIN CAMPUS

JENNIFER W. DICKEY

Charleston   London

THE
History
PRESS

Published by The History Press
Charleston, SC 29403
www.historypress.net

First published 2013

Manufactured in the United States

ISBN 978.1.62619.202.7

Library of Congress CIP data applied for.

CONTENTS

FOREWORD

Strong community is formed by powerful common experiences, as when people survive a flood or fight together in battle. When they emerge on the other side, this shared experience becomes the basis for a deep, permanent bond that is stronger than blood.
—*Tim Keller*

This book tells the story of a bold experiment—an educational initiative designed to disrupt the generational poverty and neglect that defined rural hamlets and farmsteads of the South after the Civil War. By every important measure, the experiment was a success, garnering national and international attention for its innovative and enterprising nature.

The working hypothesis was that a residential education that fused academic, spiritual and practical dimensions could create a gate of opportunity for young men and women otherwise mired in an unforgiving cycle of hopelessness. The aim was to invest in the region's most precious natural resources—its young people—to transform them into intelligent, hardworking, moral and productive citizens. The vision was that these young people would in turn establish families and communities on which the future of the region could be built. The woman with this remarkable vision—and the determination to make it a reality—was Martha Berry.

Martha began this endeavor as a thirty-seven-year-old woman with no college education, no fundraising experience, no business know-how and no experience directing a residential school of this sort. There was no obvious source of support for the school she envisioned, certainly not in a South that was still recovering from the ravages of the Civil War. Naysayers abounded, and her own family was skeptical, quite sure that her stubborn foolishness would end in failure. And as this account makes plain, there were failures along the way. But those failures, and the lessons they provided, combined with Martha's unflagging spirit, yielded successes beyond imagination.

Her vision and work were embedded in the needs of a specific moment and time. It is important to understand that at the turn of the twentieth century, only 25 percent of students nationally graduated from high school. No public high schools existed in northwest Georgia, and the state did not fund a seven-month school year until 1937. By 1952, the number of students graduating from a high school in Georgia had increased to nearly 60 percent, and that number increased to over 75 percent in the years between 1963 and 1972 before beginning a slight decline.

As society changed during the twentieth century, the Berry Schools also evolved in a multifaceted way with separate schools for elementary children, high school boys, high school girls, older boys and, eventually, a college. This book focuses primarily on the Mount Berry School for Boys, located on Berry's mountain campus, and its successor academy. Always close to Martha Berry's heart, this school existed in various forms for nearly seventy-five years.

Martha's experiment unfolded during her lifetime and continued in the decades after her death in 1942 under the leadership of talented teachers and staff. This story is equally a story about their resolve and resiliency. Although the high school closed in 1983 to give way to a sole focus by Berry on education at the college level, this is not the story of a school that died. The high school lives on in the "head, heart and hands" of its graduates.

At its core, this book is their story. Schools often point to those alumni who achieved material and business success as evidence of their own success, and certainly the Berry high school can claim many such alumni. Roy Richards (1930), at only twenty-five, started what became one of the world's largest wire and cable manufacturing companies. Smith Foster (1949) was a leader in the tufted carpet industry. Gene Anderson (1963) was a principal partner of one of the region's largest property-management firms. The list of such successes is a compelling one.

But at a place where work of all varieties was considered worthwhile and where service to others was the watchword, high school graduates across generations rose to leadership in many callings. They were able to "punch above their weight." The Reverend Luis Leon (1967), who came to Berry as a "Pedro Pan" refugee from Cuba, has served as a clergyman to multiple presidents of both parties as rector of St. John's Episcopal Church across from the White House, the "Church of the Presidents." Jerry Davis (1961) has served as president of Alice Lloyd College and College of the Ozarks, both with strong work traditions like Berry. Angela Dickey (1975), sister of the author, has served among the higher ranks of our nation's diplomats, having had postings in Asia, the Middle East and other parts of the world. And even in avocations, alumni have excelled: Don Jones (1950), a former Emory University dean, has judged every major dog show in the country, including the Westminster Kennel Club dog show, as well as competitions around the globe.

The high school, reflecting its founder, saw great potential in young people that others overlooked. Eugene Gunby (1919) proved his mettle despite terrible disability from polio, going on from Berry to become an accomplished lawyer and judge—and an avid horseman. And Jimmy Fletcher (1964), severely disabled by cerebral palsy in his movement and his ability to talk, inspired all who knew him with his grit and determination to overcome those limits. He was his class's valedictorian. While these and hundreds more alumni benefited from the "intangible magic" of the high school, they also came to embody that magic.

The Mount Berry School for Boys and Berry Academy live on today as the foundation for Berry College, a top-tier liberal arts institution that would not exist without its high school progenitor. The residential nature of the college and its extensive work program were built on the foundation of the high school model, and a number of the high school graduates also received degrees from the college.

Today, a college education is more readily available and a college degree more likely than a high school diploma was during the foundational years of the Berry high school. For a good part of its history and for many of its students, the Berry high school was the last stop for young people before entering society as responsible adult citizens. In the United States, that moment of transition has thankfully shifted from high school graduation to college graduation, as Martha Berry presciently foresaw when she founded a junior college twenty-four years after starting her initial school.

The same values that the Mount Berry School for Boys and Berry Academy aimed to instill in high school students, Berry College aims to instill in its graduates by means of a threefold education of the "head, heart and hands." The grade level has shifted, the school has matured and society has changed dramatically. But the vision of Berry endures: to produce life-ready graduates fully prepared to improve the communities in which they live, work and serve. This vision transcends curricular focus and grade level as it is worked out again and again in successive decades. Yet the spirit of Berry endures, as is evident in the shared values, common experiences and easy interactions today among all Berry alumni, college and high school alike.

In commissioning this book, I chose another distinguished graduate of the high school to tell the story. Jennifer Dickey, a 1977 graduate, knows Berry, and she knows the high school. The daughter of two of Berry's most beloved faculty and staff members, she is an accomplished public historian. She has also served previously as director of Oak Hill and the Martha Berry Museum.

She was charged to tell the story of the high school in a factual and unvarnished fashion, knowing full well that there are, in the midst of the joy and laughter in these pages, also moments of pain and hurt, as is true in any life story. Perhaps the most hurtful such moment was the decision to close Berry Academy in 1983. For some, it was an apparent moment of betrayal; for others, it was the inevitable and appropriate conclusion to an experiment that had run its course. While painful, it is important to tell the story in whole—the good, bad and ugly—so that the high school can shine rightfully as a central part of the history of Berry and its contribution to the communities of the region.

In my years at Berry, I have been amazed at the intensity of the emotional response regarding the Mount Berry School for Boys and its successor academy. Every year, hundreds of alumni crowd into Hill Dining Hall to visit one another and to honor former teachers, coaches, administrators and classmates. The high school has been closed now for thirty years, yet many of these graduates are moved deeply by events that occurred four and five decades ago. Clearly, the high school had an effect that lives on.

But what is it that still fuels the intensity of emotion for Mount Berry School for Boys? In part, perhaps, it is the nostalgia that we all feel for the years of our youth, a formative time when our lives were uncharted, full of dreams and still before us. For many of the high school boys, however, the years at Berry were not entirely pleasant. They were separated from family during these trying years. Many came from difficult home circumstances. Although the setting was picturesque, the day-to-day life itself was demanding and the rules restricting. Adolescent boys living, working, eating, worshipping and studying together, week after week, resulted in a lot of hilarity and an equal amount of hellishness. The reality was often harsh and not something that would be condoned today. One respected graduate speaks tearfully of the band of brothers forged in this fire. It is likely the nature of this shared experience that serves as the basis for a deep, permanent bond that is stronger than blood.

I am pleased that the story of the Mount Berry School for Boys and its successor academy is finally being told in such a comprehensive way. My friend Tom Butler talks of the "intangible magic" that was the high school—a recurring theme of this book. But as the story makes plain, the magic of the high school was not just intangible; it was inextinguishable.

STEPHEN BRIGGS
President, Berry College

PREFACE

The desire by the high school alumni to create this very special book came from the realization that the history and mystique of our beloved school were quickly slipping away into the vapor of time. While we certainly wished that a history of this powerful educational institution could have been written two decades ago, a worthwhile history by its nature requires patience and distance. The events that transpired to cause this book to be written are documented below.

In the winter of 2006–07, several of us met at the Alumni Center over a four-month period to plan a tribute banquet for our beloved coach Jerry Shelton. During our work together, we rekindled strong connections from days gone by, as well as our deep, undeniable love for the unique Berry history we all shared.

We also became keenly aware of the fact that since the closing of the school in 1983, there had been a quiet, but steady erosion of the important signs and symbols of the high school, so much so that most of the college students were only vaguely aware that there had ever even been a high school at Berry. Without knowing it, they were living and walking on hallowed ground that deserved deep, joyful reverence.

After Coach Shelton's tribute in March 2007, three of us (Bob Williams, '62H, John Shahan, '64A and I, '65A) met for an early breakfast the following month to wrap up a few last details of the celebration. We had ancient history and enjoyed working together and with others on this Berry project. Because of our shared experiences, we knew ourselves as brothers and agreed we would never again let our Berry family be neglected.

We also vowed we would not allow something as sacred as Berry's glorious high school history to die the whimpering death we were witnessing without proper commemoration. We instinctively knew that our small group was in a fortuitous position to advance an awareness of this decay and find a way to gather and preserve the bones and stories as a legacy for present and future generations. We had never had a path for closure, and we each still felt grief from the sudden demise of our school in 1983. Witnessing firsthand the apparent apathy toward our school's history, we could see that with each year that passed, it was one more nail in the coffin of memories. We decided it was time to do something to tell the gripping story of what happened at the bottom of that old mountain. We had to create a plan to ensure that the grandeur of this magnificent educational experience would not fade into oblivion.

Three crucial steps were taken: 1) we continued to gather in Rome every month over breakfast to better organize ourselves and establish clear, workable goals; 2) we connected with Berry's Office of Alumni Affairs for guidance and assistance; and 3) we began the process of reaching out to as many of our brothers and sisters of Berry as possible in an effort to strengthen our force and influence.

Once the word circulated about what we were doing, those who could make it started coming to the meetings to support the tasks ahead, and those who could not attend waved the flag, sent money and cheered us on. The secondary benefit for all of us was that it was profoundly meaningful to simply spend time with people who shared our same Berry blood, no matter our class, age or gender, and from that we all drew strength to press on.

We officially adopted the name the Berry Breakfast Club, and we developed one simple mission: preserve the history of Martha Berry's educational high school model from its inception in 1902 to its closing in 1983.

We set three strategic objectives: 1) request that Dr. Briggs, Berry's new president, address the closing of the academy in the quarterly alumni publication *Berry Magazine*, acknowledging that the abrupt manner in which the high school was closed had regrettably hurt and alienated alumni and students; 2) create space somewhere in the museum or campus proper dedicated to the display of high school pictures and memorabilia; and 3) have a candid book written about the history of the high school, the stories from the students still living and all the events that led to the doors closing on Miss Berry's original dream.

On September 8, 2007, Dr. Steve Briggs agreed to meet with us so that we could talk with him and present our objectives. He had become Berry's eighth president on July 1, 2006, and had just finished his first year in office. We hoped he would endorse and support what we felt were very important actions necessary to breathe life back into this large group of orphaned alumni. We had heard great things about him and felt our chances were good for him at least to hear us out and then ponder the merits of our proposal. We were not disappointed. He had an easy way about him and immediately put us at ease so that straightforward dialogue could take place.

For almost three hours, he took his valuable time to hear and consider what we had to say. We told him about the school's closing—how poorly we felt it had been done, how the high school's name had been essentially erased from the campus and how this entire process had grieved and angered most of us. We told him that because of all of this, the connection had been severed, causing any requests for gifts to become salt in the wounds.

We also told him that it was extremely important to the legacy of Berry that we document, preserve and promote the history of Miss Martha's first school, which literally had saved the lives of thousands of children since 1902. And to our great joy, he got it. He told us he understood and agreed that all of our ideas were reasonable and worthwhile. He took immediate action, and we began to exhale in anticipation of the launching of our plan.

Dr. Briggs wrote about the school's closing in an article titled "The Many and the One" in the fall 2008 issue of the *Berry Magazine*, and an article by Rick Woodall titled "The Torch Still Burns" in that same issue addressed the legacy of the high school. Over the next year, discussions were begun on the feasibility of establishing a museum display within the limited space available, and a long-range plan was begun. And then, to our delight, one of our own, Dr. Jennifer Dickey, was selected to be the writer of the book.

We had known that for a book to be written to capture fully the mystique of the student experience, the writer would need to be someone with an intimate knowledge of our school's singular history, as well as possess sensitive insight into the unrestrained passion felt by those of us who had been students of Berry. Jennifer was perfect for the task. She had literally been raised on Miss Martha's school grounds and was one of us—a sister of the clan. We were overjoyed.

Jennifer shares her extensive research of documents from various sources, including Martha Berry, President Theodore Roosevelt, Henry Ford, Dr. John Bertrand and many more who sought to actualize Miss Berry's dream. As I read the book, Jennifer's words made me feel as though

I were living in the midst of the triumphs and agonies of all those years, and I found myself crying, laughing and fuming as her words made history breathe again. Many times, I felt I was a "fly on the wall" listening to the discussions and decisions of the people who made Berry a living, breathing life form. I grieved as if I had been there when the news of Miss Martha's death struck me down, as I know it did everyone who was there at the time. What a treasure of words we have before us to be able to go back in time and discover that these were real people with real problems of the world. Martha Berry was an amazing woman, and Jennifer has brought her back to amaze and inspire us all over again.

What you are about to read is a love story. It has all the drama, passion and intrigue that would make any great novel a page-turner. It is about a masterful vision that came to life. It is about bone-weary perseverance and hard work. It is about money, politics, grief, power and the human condition. It is about believing so strongly in something that, by sheer determination, it was made to happen. It is about sacrifice, generosity and salvation. It is about a woman and her team of believers who, by the grace of God, found a way to snatch generations of children from the jaws of poverty, ignorance and despair and in so doing created new possibilities for all humanity.

Martha Berry had something special shimmering deep in her heart, planted early on by the good Lord. She gave each student part of this special something, even after her death, simply because she believed in us and because we had been anointed by the waters of her school. No one knows what this was exactly, nor did we understand how to duplicate it, but those of us who were students there are deeply familiar with the intimate hold it has on us even after all these years. It is like gold, and it is real—and it is the heart of our passion.

My only physical evidence of it is this: Each time I arrive on campus, a hush comes over me. I fall silent into myself as I do in the quiet moments before church preparing for God. I can feel the vibrations, like bees making honey in my chest, and as I arrive within that land of beauty at the foot of the old mountain, memories slip into me, one by one, reminding me of how it was and how so many of us were saved and changed forever. It is then that I remember I was one of the luckiest boys on earth to have found my way to Berry and to have lived Miss Martha's godly dream.

When our school closed in 1983, there was a collective disturbance in the souls of all of our alumni. In the process of preserving our history, we hope that this book might in some way ease the grief we all felt from the death of our school. The time will come when all of us who were students there will be gone, but now the full story will live on. All who read this will know that something truly miraculous happened at the bottom of that mountain. With the touch of God and laser-focused determination, anything is possible.

The Berry Breakfast Club would like to thank our hero, Dr. Steve Briggs, and all of his staff for listening to us and finding a way to have this book written. We want to thank Chris Watters, Director of Alumni Relations, and her staff for their generous time and guidance to help make this book a reality. We want to thank Jerry Shelton for his support and advice during the process of this endeavor. And we especially want to thank Dr. Jennifer Dickey for agreeing to be our writer and for creating something as powerful as this amazing book. When I read this manuscript, I believed Miss Martha was looking over my shoulder. I also believe she wrote on the front page in bright red ink: "A+. Well done, Jennifer. Well done."

TOM BUTLER
Class of '65, Berry Academy
President, Berry Breakfast Club

Acknowledgements

As the author of this book, I owe a great debt to many people who made it possible. Members of the Berry Breakfast Club, high school alumni who meet once a month, provided the impetus for greater recognition of the history of the high school that operated for more than six decades on the mountain campus, a history that is often overshadowed by that of Berry College. Berry College president Stephen Briggs recognized the importance of this history and what it meant to so many alumni and agreed that a book that focused primarily on the history of the operations on the mountain campus was in order. On behalf of President Briggs, Chief of Staff Alexander (Whit) Whitaker asked me to write this book. Whit made sure that I had unfettered access to files in the president's office that helped me tell the story, especially those related to the final years of the school's operation. Whit's patience, combined with his constant encouragement and ongoing support, was instrumental in allowing me to carry out my research and complete this project.

Archivist Michael O'Malley allowed me to peruse the vast resources of the Berry College Archives, and the student workers at the Archives helped enormously with making copies and scanning photographs. Madeline Briggs was a great help in identifying photographs. All of the photographs are from the collection of the Berry College Archives unless otherwise noted.

The high school alumni, faculty and staff who agreed to participate in oral history interviews for this project were extremely generous with their time and their stories. Their willingness to contribute their memories has certainly helped me understand the significance of the high school in a different way. Even though not all of their voices appear in this book, they certainly inform the story. I would especially like to thank Dr. William Scheel, who despite some misgivings agreed to talk with me about the final year of the academy's operation. The closing of Berry Academy was a particularly painful time for him, something he had locked away. I hope our discussions proved to be as cathartic for him as writing this book has been for me.

I was fortunate to have a great support team for conducting the oral history interviews. Ouida Dickey, Carolyn Smith, Harlan Chapman, Frank Adams, Kathy Knapp and several students from the alumni office assisted with conducting and recording the interviews. Aaron Jermundson and students in the Berry College Multimedia Services Center lent me video-recording equipment and converted tapes to DVDs.

In addition to conducting numerous oral history interviews, Ouida Dickey supported this project in a variety of ways. She served as a research assistant, always willing to dig through files in the archives to help me plug the gaps in my research materials. She read each chapter multiple times, making sure that every comma and hyphen was in the right place and that there were no dangling participles to be found. She is the best copy editor I know, and any mistakes that remain in this book are mine alone. Throughout this project, she encouraged and inspired me in a way that only a mother can.

Kathy Knapp has served as a sounding board, reader, research assistant, videographer and all-around provider of moral support as I worked my way through this project. She has read the manuscript countless times and offered helpful advice that has greatly improved the final product. My sister, Angela Dickey, and my dear friend Faith Gay, with whom I lived through some of the history that I have recounted in this book, both shared their memories of our high school years and offered me encouragement along the way.

I would like to thank several faculty and staff at Kennesaw State University who have patiently listened to my stories about Berry and offered their support in myriad ways. Julia Brock, Richard Harker, Catherine Lewis and David Parker have been great colleagues and friends. I consider it a privilege to work with them.

I am especially grateful to all of the alumni of the various schools of the mountain campus who contributed to this story. It is to them that I dedicate this book.

INTRODUCTION

During alumni weekend of May 2010, former students from the Mount Berry School for Boys (MBSB) gathered for a reunion in Hill Dining Hall. Grown men in their sixties became teary eyed as they reminisced about their days on the mountain campus at the MBSB. Many of them later posted their reflections online. William Kline recalled the "time when we were young and strong with our entire lives ahead of us. And a time when I had the only 'brothers' that I ever had." Kline was overwhelmed by "the intensity and nostalgia with which memories" of his time at Berry came rushing back, he wrote, and was "amazed at how powerfully it hit me when I was back on campus."[1]

Kline was among the students who helped construct the track on the mountain campus, and he recalled his first trip back to the campus in the 1990s:

> The track had nearly gone back to nature, but I could still make out the track through the grass, as well as the high jump and pole vault and long jump pits. So I started jogging around that track, all by myself. Then the memories of being strong and able to sprint all 440 yards around that track after taking the baton from my teammate on the mile relay came rushing in. Frankly, it was pretty overwhelming. Strong memories of lost youth and friendships, I guess. And I suppose that track all grown over with grass was a powerful symbol of all that has gone by. I didn't know what Berry meant to me, except maybe finally on graduation day. I always had sort of a bad attitude toward Berry and was just wanting to get out of there, I thought,

when it dawned on me that I was real close to a lot of my brothers, and there was a good chance I would never see any of them again. And for the most part, I didn't. But I remember, for a decade or more after I left Berry, maybe once every year or two, during stressful times, I would dream I was back at Berry, in one of those dorm rooms I hated, but with my friends. I guess what I would feel in those dreams was safe and secure.[2]

Kline's experience is echoed by his "brothers," who are transported back to the Berry of their youth when they return to the campus. As Jack Pigott wrote, "Every Berry reunion I go to takes me back to the decade of the '60s for an entire weekend, to a time at Berry when things were safe, certain, and secure. Unfortunately, the trip returning to the 21st century is a downer."[3]

What was so special about this school at the base of Lavender Mountain that has inspired so many people and still brings a tear to the eyes of its alumni almost three decades after the school ceased to exist? Many people are nostalgic about their high school "glory days," but alumni of the high school that operated on the mountain campus at Mount Berry, Georgia, seem to have an almost unnatural affinity for their school. This book explores the history of the school that operated on the mountain campus between 1916 and 1983—how it began, how it ended and what it has meant to those who went there.

As a 1977 graduate of the high school, I have a keen interest in both the history and the alumni of the school. I grew up on the Berry campus, the child of two professors at Berry College, Ouida and Garland Dickey. It is likely that I logged more years as a student on the Berry campus than just about anyone, having attended nursery school, middle school, high school and college at Berry. I think it is fair to say I was indoctrinated into the system. I can also honestly say that of all those years enrolled in various components of the Berry Schools, my years at Berry Academy meant the most to me. Perhaps that is to be expected—for many people, their high school years stand out as a particularly memorable time. But there was something exceptional about Berry Academy. It was a magical place. It was there that I had the good fortune to encounter educators such as Earlene Doster, who taught eighth-grade social studies, and Comer Yates, who taught history and American government. Both of them had an enormous impact on my life and taught me to love history. Perhaps the most influential person was Gary McKnight, who taught science and coached track and cross-country. I was never much of a scientist, but Coach McKnight instilled in me a love for running that still motivates me today. Hardly a day goes by that I don't think of him and am grateful for the role he played in my life.

The magic began back in 1902, when Martha Berry first opened the doors of Berry Academy's predecessor—the Boys Industrial School—on eighty-three acres on what is today the residential end of the main campus. She began that first semester with five boys. In 1916, she began operating the Mount Berry Farm School at the base of Lavender Mountain. The Mount Berry Farm School was a short-lived experiment that soon became the Foundation School. Between 1916 and 1925, the boys enrolled at the school on the mountain campus constructed numerous buildings. During the 1925–26 school year, Friendship Hall was built twice after it burned to the ground shortly before completion.

At the beginning of the 1926–27 school year, big changes were afoot as Berry added college-level courses to its curriculum. The launching of Berry College led to the migration of the freshman and sophomore high school boys, who had attended the Berry School on the lower campus, to the mountain campus. Berry College had a mere twenty students enrolled during its first year of operation. By its second year, the college boasted an enrollment of over one hundred. By 1930, when the college had evolved from a two-year to a four-year program, the entire boys' high school operation had moved to the mountain campus, and the name of the school was changed to the Mount Berry School for Boys, or MBSB, as it was known around campus. Another dormitory (Pilgrim Hall) was built, and work soon began on what would become one of the most modern and picturesque dairy facilities in the Southeast: the Normandy Barns.

Over the next thirty-three years, the Mount Berry School for Boys offered an educational opportunity to boys who were willing to work their way through. During that time, the Possum Trot School opened and closed twice, the Foundation School ceased to exist and the Martha Berry School for Girls, the girls' high school begun by Martha Berry in 1909, was phased out. The board of trustees agonized over the decision to close the Martha Berry School for Girls, fearing that alumni and friends might react badly, especially since it was the one school that bore Miss Berry's name. Ultimately, the declining enrollment of high school girls and a pressing need for more space for college women led to a phased closure of the school that was completed by 1956. Above the archway at the Ford Building, carved in stone, is a reminder of this branch of the institution that is no longer with us: the Martha Berry School for Girls. Most people pass under the archway and never look up or notice this piece of history.

Another change occurred on the mountain campus in 1964, when the Mount Berry School for Boys became Berry Academy. Although the work program continued to be a hallmark of the school, the focus was now unabashedly college preparatory, as noted in the new catalogue.

Over the next two decades, more changes occurred at Berry Academy—the school became coeducational, a middle school was added, Hamrick Hall burned for the second time and was reconstructed and the work program became what one of my classmates described as a "shadowy remnant" of its former self. I graduated in the spring of 1977 from the academy, and like many of the high school students before me, I enrolled in Berry College. In the late fall of 1982, I was in graduate school in Columbia, South Carolina, when I received a phone call from my mother, who was still on the faculty at Berry, informing me that the board of trustees had announced that the academy would be closed at the end of the 1982–83 school year. I was in a state of disbelief. This was my school—my favorite school of all time.

Like many of my fellow alumni, I was heartbroken about the closing of this institution that had played such an enormous role in my life. Rumors swirled about what would become of the Berry Academy physical plant. There was talk of developing it into a corporate retreat—a prospect that pleased almost no one. In February 1983, the board of trustees developed a set of guidelines for the use of the former high school facilities that included the requirement that the use of the facilities "must be compatible with Berry College and its mission" and stated that the facilities were not for sale.[4] By the fall of 1983, development director John Lipscomb reported that the "person indicating the most enthusiastic interest" in the high school facilities was Truett Cathy, founder and owner of Chick-fil-A.[5] Mr. Cathy had made his first visit to the school in 1982 as a guest speaker in the Olin Entrepreneur Lecture Series. Soon, everyone was talking about how the high school campus was going to become Chicken U.

In September 1984, the *Campus Carrier* announced the opening of the WinShape Centre. Underwritten by Chick-fil-A, the WinShape Centre would serve as a residential campus for college students who had worked at Chick-fil-A while they were in high school and who now qualified for a scholarship to attend Berry College. Like many of my former classmates, I had mixed emotions about this development. While I was glad the buildings would not be mothballed and that there were students living in the dorms again, I was skeptical about this new program for this group of students who came to be known as the "chicken kids." For the next twenty-three years, I carried with me mixed feelings about Berry. On the one hand, it was the place I had grown up—it was home. On the other hand, the high school that I loved so much had been closed.

As luck would have it, in the late summer of 2004, I found myself back at Berry in a new capacity—I had accepted the position as curator at Oak Hill and the Martha Berry Museum. I was still unhappy about the academy's closing, and I still did not fully understand or embrace the WinShape operation out on the mountain campus, but I came back anyway. Then, several of the "chicken kids" came to work for me at the museum. Whenever they would talk about living on the mountain campus, I would see the same spark in their eyes that I used to feel about the place.

I began to interact with the staff of the WinShape Centre, and soon I was invited to give a talk on the history of the Normandy Barns at the WinShape Retreat. The staff members were so excited to learn a bit about the history of the buildings where they worked, and their enthusiasm for the place was contagious. I got to know Dan and Bubba Cathy, whose conviction and devotion to this place that I loved so much was clearly evident. I began to reevaluate my position on this mountain campus operation. After all, the Cathy family was doing exactly what Martha Berry had done one hundred years earlier: making it possible for young men and women to receive an education at this extraordinary place. The Cathys and the "chicken kids" loved it just as I loved it.

Many alumni of Berry's high school still lament the closing of their school just as I did for so many years. While this book is unlikely to soothe their anger about the loss of something they consider so precious, I hope it will at least help them understand a bit more about the history of the institution. The high school operation at Berry was dynamic. It evolved through the years as circumstances dictated—both during Martha Berry's lifetime and after her death. The educational institution that closed in May 1983 was vastly different from the institution that Martha Berry opened in 1902. Yet undergirding the ongoing operations at what is now Berry College is the spirit of the institution's founder.

Writing this book has been a cathartic experience. While conducting my research, I encountered alumni from the school's history from the 1930s to the last year of the school's operation in 1983. I was struck by how devoted these alumni were to their high school and how sad, and sometimes angry, many of them still were almost three decades after the closing. As one alumnus explained, there was "an intangible magic" about the place. Many memories of the school's history may be lost in the tall grass, much like the track at the end of the "Stretch," but there remains a trace of the school that meant so much to so many of us over the years. What follows is the story of a piece of Martha Berry's institution that for many of us remains the most magical of places.

Chapter 1

A Most Worthy Institution

Miss Berry is doing one of the greatest practical works for American citizenship
that has been done within a decade.
—Theodore Roosevelt

On January 10, 1902, Miss Martha Berry placed an advertisement in the *Rome Tribune* announcing that an "Industrial School for Boys" would open on January 13, 1902, with a course of study that included "literacy, industrial and business training." Board and tuition would cost ten dollars per month. The aim of the school was "to place the pupils under the most refining home influences, and to fit them to be useful citizens."[6] The Sunday, January 12 edition of the *Rome Tribune* offered a lengthy article on what it deemed a "Most Worthy Institution," noting that the opening of the school marked "the beginning of new and better things for the section in which the school is planned" and offering a "strong and cordial endorsement" of the school.

On the day following the grand opening, the *Tribune* gave "its highest endorsement to Miss Martha Berry's Industrial School for Boys which opened yesterday with bright prospects of doing grand work for the good of this section."[7] The newspaper reported that Miss Berry knew "from experience and close observation the needs of certain classes of our boys" and that the school represented one of the "noblest institutions this section of the south has ever known."[8] The *Atlanta Constitution* offered equally effusive praise of Miss Berry's "noble work," adding that her school was "designed to give worthy poor boys a Christian education at a minimum cost" and that "Eastern philanthropists are interested in her plans, and it is more than probable that she will receive handsome endowments to aid in her noble work."[9]

The effusive praise bestowed on Martha Berry and her fledgling school at its opening in 1902 was prescient. Over the next three decades, Berry's noble work would expand to include a school for girls, an elementary school, a junior college and a senior college, all of which adhered to Berry's initial philosophy of training the rural poor to become useful citizens by educating them and exposing them to the "most refining home influences." Fundamental to the operation of her school was the notion that the students would work for their educations.

Prior to opening her boarding school, Berry had operated a series of day schools in Floyd County. Attendance by the day students was spotty at best. Many of the students had to travel over dirt roads and pathways to get to the school. During inclement weather, these routes were often impassable. All of the students resided on small farms, and during planting and harvesting seasons, their efforts were sorely needed on the farm. Several years of running her day schools convinced Martha Berry that the only way she could really make an impact on the lives of the rural poor was through the establishment of a boarding school that removed the boys from the daily demands of working on their family farms and placed them in an environment where they received training in the fundamentals of reading, writing and arithmetic and the use of the latest scientific farming techniques, along with a big dose of etiquette and Christian character.

In its second year of operation, the Boys Industrial School, as it was originally called, was heralded as a "unique success" by the *Atlanta Constitution* for its application of the new "idea of practical and industrial, versus theoretical and academic education." Reporter James A. Hall wrote, "To take the poor country boy who has had no opportunity to educate himself and make of him the very best man and most useful member of society of which he is capable of making is the aim and hope of the school." By the end of the first spring term in 1903, the school had fifty students and six teachers, according to Hall, with each student paying only five dollars a month for board. The school was a world unto itself, with each student's "personal conduct as well as his intellectual and moral training under the constant care and guidance of the faculty."[10]

According to the *Atlanta Constitution*, the Boys Industrial School became known as "a school that teaches by doing," with the boys undertaking all the work necessary to operate the institution, from growing the crops and

Left: Martha Berry, circa 1900.

Below: Editorial staff of the Boys Industrial School newspaper, the *Berry School Advance*, 1904.

Students building the Recitation Hall, 1904.

Farming was fundamental to the work program, 1915.

livestock that fed them to constructing the buildings in which they lived, worked and studied.[11] Everyone was expected to do his fair share of the work. As one student explained, "If a boy comes here and is slothful and unwilling to do his share, we make it so hot for him that he is soon only too glad to get away."[12]

From the beginning, Martha Berry struggled to make ends meet. Many of the boys were not able to afford even the ten dollars a month room, board and tuition that the school charged. The work done by the boys kept a roof over their heads and kept them fed, but it did not cover the expenses associated with running the school, such as salaries for the teachers. By the beginning of the school's second year of operation, the school had become well known in the area, but the school's success had not translated into a financial windfall for the institution, and according to Berry, there was a pressing need to expand the school's facilities. She noted:

> *The desire of country boys to enter it is constantly spreading, but the school income does not increase accordingly. It grieves me to refuse a boy when he comes to me with $20 and says he has been saving it for three years to go to school, and that since he can pay his way and is willing to work I must take him in. When another comes many miles up the river, and his boat breaking down half way he walks the rest in his eagerness to reach the school, I would do anything to admit him, but there is no room.*[13]

Martha Berry recognized that she needed outside financial support in order to keep her school operating. According to the *Atlanta Constitution*, by 1907, the school faced an annual deficit of $10,000, in spite of "the generosity of the good people of Georgia and of the grateful graduates of the school."[14] Berry began taking what she called "begging trips" in an effort to raise money for the school. As a member of high society, Berry had connections that she was able to leverage to make contacts with potential donors. Armed with an album full of photographs of the boys and her school, she embarked on trips to the Northeast to tell the story of her "educational oasis for the poor boys of Georgia."[15]

It was on such a trip to Washington, D.C., in 1907 that Martha Berry met President Theodore Roosevelt. Determined to make the best of what she assumed would be a short audience with the president in his White House office, Berry began to tell Roosevelt about her school and showed him pictures of the boys. "I could see that the story of my struggle and the struggle which many of the boys were making appealed to him," she

Berry School student Joe Lane, circa 1914.

later recalled. According to Berry, the president became so enthralled with her story that when his secretary informed him that a senator had arrived for a meeting, Roosevelt responded, "Let him wait! This school is the real thing, and I must know more about it." After half an hour, Roosevelt offered to host a dinner in Martha Berry's honor, explaining that he could not give her much money but that he could provide her with "friends and influence" of those who would be willing to help the school. Roosevelt hosted the dinner at which Martha Berry told the story of her school. Berry recounted that "nearly all of the guests sent contributions to the school, and some of them [became] our good and constant friends."[16] Roosevelt himself contributed money for a scholarship and pledged to visit the school one day. In a letter written shortly before he left the White House, Roosevelt stated, "There is no school in the south in which I take more interest than in the Berry School, for it is, in very fact, what its title denotes, a Christian industrial school for poor country boys," adding that his only regret was that Berry had no school for girls.[17]

Martha Berry's begging trips began to bear fruit. In 1909, Andrew Carnegie and Mrs. Olivia Sage, a noted New York philanthropist and widow of railroad magnate Russell Sage, each pledged $25,000 to the school if Berry could raise an additional $50,000.[18] By the spring of 1909, the school had grown from two buildings on 83 acres to include six buildings on 1,400 acres, and Martha Berry had plans for further expansion. Encouraged by the support of Theodore Roosevelt, Carnegie, Sage and others, Berry

Students and staff welcoming former president Teddy Roosevelt at the Recitation Hall, 1910.

opened the Martha Berry School for Girls approximately one mile north of the boys' school in November 1909.

The first building constructed for the girls' school was a two-story log building named Louise Hall after Mrs. Louise Inman of Atlanta. Louise Hall was constructed by the boys, who had been encouraged to support the efforts of the girls' school at their spring commencement ceremony. "You young scamps, if you are worth anything at all, you will scratch around and get an education for yourself. But the country girls—your sisters—they are the ones who need help," the boys were told. The June 1916 issue of the *Southern Highlander*, the school's fundraising magazine, reminded its readers of the "shut-in lives and narrow outlook of the country girls and especially of the mountain girls. The boy can push his way out into the world; a hundred avenues are open to him; he needs but ambition and energy. But the girl—what does life have to offer her?" Readers were reminded that American civilization had done little to improve conditions for the "country girl," who customarily was not allowed to "venture far beyond the pale of the home" and who was offered a future that held "nothing better than her mother knew—drudgery, loneliness, a hard and shut-in life." Education

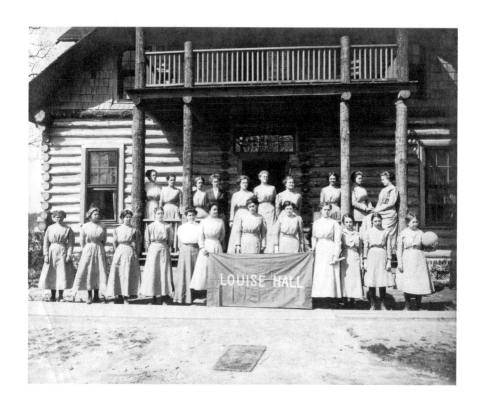

was "the channel" through which country girls could reap the "benefits of those mighty forces of progress which have revolutionized the lot but not the character of her more fortunate sisters."

The aim of the Martha Berry School for Girls was "not to take the girls out of the home but to prepare them for happy and useful lives in the home... to train mountain girls for home-making—to bring into their lives sweetness and light; by the inculcation of right methods of work and right ideals of service to take away the drudgery and bring in the joy of the home duties, and by the cultivation of mind and spirit to prepare for the divinely given privileges of the home."[19] The program at the girls' school, much like that at the boys' school, combined a traditional education with practical instruction in home economics and religion. "The life of the school [was] that of an ideal Christian family, of which the students are members, each having her duties to perform, her place in the family circle to fill, and all under the care and guidance of cultured Christian women."[20]

All of the girls worked. They cooked and served the meals, made their own clothes, kept the house, did laundry and tended the cows, chickens and gardens. The girls paid twenty-five dollars per four-month term. They lived on the second floor of Louise Cottage and attended classes on the ground floor. A second, one-room ramshackle building near Louise Cottage, known as Sunshine Shanty, served as the classroom and work space for the girls' school handicrafts program—a program that Martha Berry began in 1910 as part of an effort to preserve the traditional crafts of the mountain people and to produce handicrafts products that were used by the students and offered for sale to the public. Reporter John Corrigan Jr. wrote that "despite the great work being done for the boys, I seriously doubt whether a greater work is not being done for the girls." As Dr. John E. White of Atlanta had recently commented, "Educate a boy, and you have an educated citizen. Educate a girl, and you have an educated family." Martha Berry's schools were taking "the boys and girls who were growing up like weeds in the flatwoods of Floyd and developing them into good citizens," according to Corrigan, "turning the inept and hopeless into the educated and aggressive citizen."[21]

Opposite, top: Students of the Martha Berry School for Girls in front of Louise Cottage, 1910.

Opposite, bottom: Students of the Berry School building Rome Cottage for the Martha Berry School for Girls, 1914.

Students of the Berry School, circa 1908.

Opposite, top: Boys in the library of the Berry School Recitation Hall, circa 1910.

Opposite, bottom: The Berry School Band marching from Blackstone Hall under the watchful eye of Martha Berry, 1918.

Whether the rural poor of north Georgia were "inept and hopeless" as Corrigan claimed, there is no question that Martha Berry's schools provided an opportunity for boys and girls who might not have otherwise had access to an education. The Georgia Constitution of 1877 "provided for 'a thorough system' of public education separate by race," but that system included nothing more than primary schools with a school term of less than six months. Although larger towns and cities often supported public schools at the primary level as well, neither the state nor the local governments provided public secondary schools.[22] Martha Berry's schools were unique in the northwest Georgia area because, unlike other private schools in the area such as the Darlington School, which opened in 1905, the Berry Schools accepted only poor students from rural areas.

Campus life at Berry was described in official school publications as "truly pleasant and educative." Students were afforded daily contact "with many other young men of noble purpose who are working for their education, and

with the teachers whose desire is to give the students the best training possible." Living arrangements at the school resulted in "close, constant, personal touch between teachers and pupils" as teachers became "trusted friends and advisors" of the students. Indeed, there was little opportunity for the students to escape the watchful eye of their teachers since the teachers lived in the dormitories and ate in the dining hall with the students.[23]

By the mid-1910s, Martha Berry's schools had grown to encompass over three thousand acres and included the Berry School, as the Boys' Industrial School had been called since 1908; the Martha Berry School for Girls; and a four-grade primary school that catered primarily to the faculty and staff of the high school operations. Among the recently acquired acreage of the school was land at the base of Lavender Mountain, some five miles from the boys' high school. In 1915, Martha Berry hired Grady Hamrick, a 1912 graduate of the Berry School, to take six boys to the land at the base of Lavender Mountain and begin construction on a log building that would serve as a dormitory for the next unit of her school system. That unit, originally known as the Mount Berry Farm School, opened in January 1916. Its creation marks the beginning of the development of the area that is today known as the mountain campus.

Chapter 2
DOING GOD'S WORK

We must keep Grady for the Mountain School this year, if possible. The school there will be a great asset to us.
—Martha Berry

A notice in the *Alumni Quarterly* in November 1915 announced "An Opportunity for Ten Boys to Earn an Education." This new unit of the Berry Schools, referred to initially as the Mount Berry Farm Settlement, was scheduled to open on January 1, 1916. The farm settlement would begin with ten boys and increase to twenty as soon as buildings were available. Lands were to be "cleared, buildings erected and all work done by 'work students.'" These students were expected to work from four to twelve months, with their wages "payable in the form of tuition, board and expenses at the Berry School during the terms following the period of work." Country boys who were at least sixteen years old, had no other means of support and were deemed eligible for admission to the Berry School were eligible for admission to the Farm Settlement. The Farm Settlement workers were expected to attend classes on the mountain campus in the evenings and Sunday church services with the students of the boys' school on the lower campus.[24]

Grady Hamrick was barely older than the work students under his supervision when he was placed in charge of the Farm Settlement operation at the base of Lavender Mountain in 1915. Following his graduation from the Berry School in 1912, Hamrick attended a business school in Atlanta for a year before being summoned back to Berry to serve as assistant bookkeeper.

Less than a year later, Martha Berry asked Hamrick "to go to Lavender Mountain and begin a school for boys in the grammar grades," recalled Hamrick. "I found out later that she had interviewed a dozen other alumni and had offered each the job, but each one turned it down, saying their wives thought it was too far from civilization for them to live. As I was single then, I could not give that excuse."[25]

On direction from Martha Berry, Hamrick and six boys traveled to the mountain campus with instructions to construct a log building that would serve as a dorm and classroom space for the new school. Hamrick and his crew lived in what he described as "an old shack which had been abandoned by the family of an old moonshiner." According to Hamrick:

> *The moonshiner, himself, had been killed in a feud with other bootleggers who lived over the ridge beyond Chestnut Cove. The place of the still was only a few hundred feet away from the old house and we could have put it in operation intact and operated it, but our mission was not that. We had come to bring Christianity and light into the dark places, build a farm and study Agriculture so that we could become useful men in the community from which we came.*[26]

Much like Martha Berry, Hamrick believed the schools were doing God's work.

The new school opened under the name of the Mount Berry Farm School with an enrollment of ten boys on January 4, 1916.[27] According to the 1916–17 catalogue, the Mount Berry Farm School was created "in order to furnish work for more boys who apply to the Berry School to work their way through." The new building, Pine Lodge, could accommodate about twenty-five boys; plans were afoot to build roads and barns for the livestock and to cultivate a farm of about five hundred acres. During the day, the boys carried out what was described as "practical farm work," and in the evenings five nights a week they received instruction in agriculture, arithmetic, English, reading and spelling. They were expected to attend the Farm School for four months, after which time "whatever each has earned will be to his credit to pay for board and tuition at the Berry School." Hamrick lived in Pine Lodge with the boys, and great effort was "put forth to make the farm work practical and the school life homelike." On Sundays, the boys from the Farm School were transported to the lower campus, where they attended church services with the students of the Berry School.[28]

The admission standards for boys at the Farm School were the same as those for the Berry School—applicants had to live in the country, be at least

Grady Hamrick and the boys of the Mount Berry Farm School on the porch of Pine Lodge, 1918.

sixteen years old, be unable to afford to attend school elsewhere and "furnish satisfactory evidence of physical, mental, and moral soundness."[29] The "aim of the Berry School," for which the Farm School was envisioned as a feeder system, was to "develop efficient Christian manhood by affording to worthy boys and young men of limited means, from rural districts, the opportunity to earn an education combining mental, moral and industrial training." According to the *Berry Schools Bulletin*, the Berry School was "neither a reformatory nor a trade school, though thorough and practical industrial courses are given." No city boys were accepted, and the "primary purpose" of the school was to train "young men for country life." Students "learned by doing," according to the catalogue, and in an effort to keep the students on the right moral path, the school required them to study the Bible daily.[30]

Martha Berry firmly believed in the notion of "training young men for country life," as she reiterated in a letter to board chairman John Eagan in September 1916 following a visit to Mentone, Alabama, where her family had a summer home. "I visited Sand Mountain and renewed my acquaintance with the mountain people," wrote Berry, "and I felt more strongly than ever the need of educating the boys and girls to go back home to teach, preach and be country doctors." On her trip over Sand Mountain, Berry "saw so many boys and girls who could not possibly come except as work students," she reported, adding that "the work boys and girls make our most valuable pupils and I wish that we could take more of them." According to Berry, donors to the school were more inclined to support the work students directly than they were to pay for "more teachers or to put up more buildings or make more conveniences."

Martha Berry was interested in keeping her students isolated from what she deemed the corrupting influence of the nearby city of Rome. Reports that the boys on the lower campus were coming in after curfew, some as late as eleven or twelve o'clock at night, were cause for great concern. "It is almost impossible to keep these boys so close to town, and our problems will grow as the town grows nearer to us," wrote Berry. The Farm School promised to "be a great asset to us," noted Berry, who was "more and more convinced that this school will have to be farther in the country."[31]

Although the isolation of the Mount Berry Farm School was part of the attraction for Martha Berry, she did recognize the need to have a physical connection between the various operations. "Eventually we shall have to have a road from one school to the other," she wrote in October 1916, as well as "a road up to the mountains so the boys may drive up their teams and take care of the valuable fruit which we have there."[32] The roads were to be built by the boys at the Farm School during the winter months after they had gathered the crops.

The Farm School quickly became a vital component of the institution because it developed "good work boys" who then moved on to the Berry School. Berry also characterized the Farm School as "the future safety-valve for the school" because of its remote location and its system of requiring the boys to work full time for one term before transferring to the Berry School, where they worked only sixteen hours a week while attending classes full time. "I should really like to have the schools made up of boys and girls who work one term and go to school the next. In that way we hold the pupils through the years," wrote Berry.[33]

In the fall of 1916, the *Berry School News* reported that the new group of students for the Farm School spent most of their first day on the lower campus, where they got to know "the boys at the original Berry School," before piling into a wagon for transport to the mountain campus. "By the time we reached here we were all worn out," wrote one of the boys, "and we were all soon in bed, dreaming of the ones we left at home and of training ourselves for the future welfare of the country." The students went straight to work the next morning, finishing a barn for the livestock, harvesting the summer crops and plowing the fields for the fall grain crops.[34]

As one group of boys transitioned from the Farm School to the Berry School in early 1917, ten new boys arrived on the mountain campus and began working on the new road up the mountain. Writing for the *Berry School News*, W.F. Bradley reported that most of the new boys were small, which would be "a great help to the school, for they won't eat so much as large boys, and that is what the school wants. It wants a crowd of small boys so it won't cost so much to see a large crop raised at the mountain this year and hope that Mr. Hamrick will clear enough money on this crop so that he can divide with the boys who help make it." Hamrick was teaching his small boys "a little of everything," Bradley continued, including how to cook, build roads and farm.[35]

By December 1916, Martha Berry reported that the school had received contributions totaling $1,000 for construction of the mountain road, with more donations promised. She wanted work to begin immediately on the road during the winter months while the Farm School students were available to do the work. The road would provide a connecting link from the Farm School to the fruit orchards, which by this time had over one thousand peach trees, as well as plum, cherry and apple trees. Access to the Farm School was important, not just for operational reasons, but also because visitors to the schools on the lower campus were "disappointed over the schools' being so low and flat and so close to the town," according to Berry. "It really takes the trip to the farm school and the mountain to convince them that we are not a city school."[36] Building the mountain road would "give the boys work that will show up," wrote Berry.

Although Berry had only a fraction of the estimated $5,000 needed for construction of the road, she was anxious for Hamrick and the students to begin the project. "Grady wants to begin the blowing up of stumps with dynamite and with the use of a plow or two," Berry reported to John Eagan, and she had given him instructions to proceed. "This sort of work appeals to people and the picturesqueness of Grady and the boys seems to open a generous vein."[37] Martha Berry was convinced that the Berry School would have to be moved to the mountain campus if it were to succeed in fulfilling its purpose of training young men for country life. "This is my dream and I hope to live to see it realized," she wrote, although "it would mean to raise a million dollars to move it; but all things are possible if we are doing God's work." The operation on the mountain campus was viewed as the ideal place to take people who had "large ideas and great money."[38]

By 1920, the school at the foot of Lavender Mountain was referred to as the Mountain Farm School. Martha Berry's dream of moving the boys' high school to the mountain campus was still a few years away, but her plans to build "a central highway connecting the three schools of the Berry system" began to become a reality. All faculty members contributed a day's salary, and the students each contributed a day's work in April 1920 to jump-start the project. The new road, which ran from Victory Lake on the lower campus to the mountain campus, was completed in 1923 and was named the Road of Remembrance in honor of the Berry boys killed in the world war.[39] Although hardly a "central highway" by today's standards, this new road, which is today referred to as the "Old Stretch Road," was entirely on land owned by the school and shortened the distance from the lower campus to the mountain campus by almost two miles.

A second log building, Cherokee Lodge, was constructed by the boys on the mountain campus in 1920 to serve as a dining hall and classroom facility. Whereas the original target market of the Farm School had been older boys who had neither the money nor the basic educational training necessary to enroll at the boys' high school on the lower campus, by 1920, the school was catering to younger boys and had become a preparatory school to the Berry School. The emphasis on academics increased, and the younger boys spent more time in classes and worked two hours a day, every day, six days a week. With an enrollment of thirty boys in the fall of 1920, the Mountain Farm School offered "a Christian home, care and training to smaller boys, preference being given to homeless boys," at a fee of sixty-five dollars for each four-month term.[40]

The school on the mountain campus continued to be a key component of Martha Berry's fundraising efforts into the early 1920s, and Berry made sure that Grady Hamrick and the boys put on a good show whenever visitors came to the campus. The Meacham family had given the money for the construction of Meacham Hall, a log dormitory building up the hill from Pine Lodge, in honor of their son Robert Meacham, who had died soon after returning from the world war. Shortly before the arrival of Mr. and Mrs. Standish Meacham in April 1922, Berry instructed Hamrick to "have everything at the Mountain Farm School in good order," and to "have the boys in clean overalls and blue shirts" for the Meachams' visit. Hamrick was to hang new curtains in the building and move the picture of Robert Meacham from the library on the lower campus to the living room of Meacham Hall. A small U.S. flag was to be draped above the picture at all times. During the visit, the boys were to "line up and march in" while singing

Mountain Farm School boys at Cherokee Lodge, 1920.

their Mountain Farm song.[41] No detail was to be overlooked in the effort to impress on the Meachams that their money was supporting the cause of uplifting the poor mountain boys.

Meacham Hall was not the last addition to the physical plant at the mountain campus in the 1920s. Early in the decade, Martha Berry confided in Grady Hamrick that everyone thought she was foolish to continue building a school on the mountain campus, but she intended to do it anyway. "If you will step on the plank of faith with me, we will build this school for the needs of the future," Berry told Hamrick. She then pointed to a hill that she had identified as the perfect site for a new recitation hall and another hill that she envisioned as the location for a new dining hall. Other hills were earmarked for dormitories and a chapel. "The buildings must be permanent and everlasting; they must be built of stone," Berry told Hamrick. Hamrick was placed in charge of having the students trained to quarry stone from the sides of the mountain and trained to lay the stone in the walls of the buildings—first a recitation hall, then a dining hall—that were constructed on the mountain campus between 1922 and 1923.[42] Along with the new buildings came a new name. The Farm School became known as the Foundation School in 1922.

Meacham Hall, circa 1923.

A sketch of the Foundation School Recitation Hall, 1922.

More than ninety boys were accepted at the Foundation School in the fall of 1922, and new faculty had been hired to accommodate the expanded enrollment. The *Berry News* reported that the new boys experienced "the usual amount of home sickness" but soon settled down to work. "They realized that they were to blaze a trail for others and they were determined that no one should go astray because of a dim trail." This trailblazing was both a figurative and literal charge to the boys at the Foundation School as they continued construction of the road linking the Foundation School to the lower campus. Although work and school were the top priorities for the boys, they were allowed some recreation, including the opportunity to participate in the track and field events at Berry's annual Field Day and to swim in the "fine artificial lake" on the mountain campus. The boys also formed a baseball team that competed against other schools in the area, as well as against the high school boys of the Berry School. Three literary societies were created to channel the intellectual energies of the boys.[43] A plea was issued in the campus newspaper for the donation of equipment for the science laboratory and the blacksmith shop, as well as a piano for the Foundation School, as the boys needed "music for their church and to keep them happy generally."[44]

The boys at the Foundation School were reportedly some of the hardest-working students on the Berry campus during the 1922–23 school year. In addition to continuing work on the road connecting the mountain campus to the rest of the schools, the boys worked feverishly to complete work on the new dining hall, the recitation hall and the water system. This became a point of pride for the boys, who were described in the campus newspaper as "builders" who would be able to look back with pride and say, "I helped to do that." The paper reported that the Foundation School boys were campus leaders in school spirit and that they were "not afraid to get down in the mud and 'do their bit.' What a wonderful place this would be if everyone were willing to take a part as the grammar school boys are doing. How many would be willing to work in mud ten inches deep, that the lake might be more beautiful?" Apparently, the Foundation School boys were doing all this "without a murmur," and when they left Berry, it was expected that they would have a love for the place that would "stand the severest test" because they had helped build it.[45]

The boys at the high school had constructed most of the buildings and roads on the lower campus in the early days of the school and would continue to do so until the 1950s, but apparently the young boys on the mountain campus approached their tasks with unparalleled zeal. "Work is the highway

Martha Berry and the boys with the first tractor given to the school by Henry Ford, 1922.

to happiness," Martha Berry told the students at the Foundation School in the fall of 1922, and "the spirit in which you do your work counts more than anything....At the Berry Schools you are taught to do work of all kinds. You are taught to honor work and are directed by skilled men and women. The co-ordination of the hand and head will strengthen your earning ability, your character and will enable you to render a valued service to humanity."[46] The work program, so vital to the creation of the school, would remain a hallmark of the institution for many years.

The boys continued to work throughout the 1922–23 school year and into the summer of 1923. Fifty boys remained on campus during the summer months and worked feverishly under the supervision of Grady Hamrick to complete construction of the stone dining hall that Martha Berry had envisioned only a year earlier. By the time the more than one hundred boys arrived to begin the fall term at the Foundation School, the dining hall was finished, and the recitation hall was nearly complete as well, prompting the campus newspaper to declare that the "Foundation School has progressed more than either of the other schools."[47] The old dining hall in Cherokee Lodge was converted into a dormitory with indoor plumbing, and the students reveled in their new "roomy, up-to-date dining hall that is good enough for a king."[48] With the completion of the recitation hall, students were able to hold their Sunday chapel services in the auditorium that was heralded to be "as good as could be found in Georgia."[49]

The school president, Leland Green, asked Clifford Hill, who was serving as the assistant supervisor in Blackstone Dining Hall on the lower campus, to transfer to the Foundation School to take charge of the culinary department in the new dining hall on a temporary basis. Green promised Hill that this assignment would last no more than three weeks. Hill often reflected that those three weeks were the longest in history "because the three weeks stretched into forty years." Hill ran the dining hall with an iron fist for the next four decades, alternately terrifying and inspiring the boys under his charge. He became known as "Judge" Hill to the boys, many of whom credited Hill with putting them on the right path in their youths. Hill demanded and got the most out of the boys assigned to the dining hall work detail. And although the boys feared his wrath, they also knew that he was kindhearted and could be counted on to give a boy the twelve cents required to attend the movies at the girls' school on Saturday nights.[50]

The school on the mountain campus continued to grow over the next few years. In the spring of 1924, the *Mount Berry News* featured an article that heralded the Foundation School as the "most notable achievement of the present decade" and "a supply station for turning out New South leaders." The school was improving faster than any other part of the Berry Schools, according to the newspaper.[51] A year later, the paper again heralded the school's progress and improvements from the "first habitable shanty" to the five buildings—Pine Lodge, Cherokee Lodge, Meacham Hall and the dining and recitation halls. "The Foundation school site was a desolate waste in 1916," the newspaper reminded its readers, "but stands forth today as an example of the achievement of Christian Education." In addition to the existing buildings, work was underway on a new workshop that would offer space for instruction in wood and ironworking and a barn. The farm operations on the mountain campus had expanded to include hundreds of acres of cultivated fields that produced grain and forage for the school's beef and sheep herds, as well as the Angora goats that supplied wool to the handicrafts operation at the girls' school. Enrollment at the Foundation School was 113, and the boys had woven themselves "into a strong brotherhood in which [they] were all comparatively equal sharers." The mountain campus, with its two lakes and winding roads, was linked to the two other schools by the Road of Remembrance, all of which "were built by willing hands guiding hungry minds eager for knowledge. How wondrously has God wrought, thru our beloved Founder, all the way from the 'little old log cabin' to the House of Dreams," proclaimed the newspaper.[52]

Although Berry publications lauded the beauty of the Foundation School campus, and Martha Berry continued to consider the school at the mountain campus to be a showplace for luring donors, she was unequivocal in her efforts to keep the school isolated from the outside world. She was also determined to maintain singular control over the operations of the institution. In August 1925, she reminded Grady Hamrick that no outsiders had been given "permission to go to the Foundation School and even when business friends of Berry have asked, they have been refused. I do not want the Rome people to get in the habit of using our roads and going to the Foundation School as they have. Will you please see that the gate to the Foundation School is locked every afternoon? I cannot turn Berry into a park, and I would appreciate it if you will make this an iron-clad rule."[53]

Throughout the 1925–26 school year, the Foundation School continued to thrive and expand. To accommodate the increasing enrollment, construction began in the spring of 1925 on a new dormitory built by the students out of the same native stone and in a style similar to that of the dining and recitation halls. Named Friendship Hall in honor of the friends of the school, primarily Emily Vanderbilt Hammond and her uncle, H.C. Sloane, who contributed to the building fund, the dormitory was expected to house eighty boys and two teachers. In the wee hours of April 20, 1926, the almost-completed building burned. The fire, which started on the first floor, quickly gutted the building, and the stone walls cracked and buckled from the heat. The loss was estimated at $65,000, and the school had insufficient insurance to cover the replacement cost. Shortly thereafter, the *Mount Berry News* reported that students and faculty from all three of the Berry Schools had made small contributions toward the reconstruction of the building, declaring that "Friendship Hall must be rebuilt! Phoenix-like she must rise from those ashes still more beautiful than before."[54] Friendship Hall was rebuilt and finally opened in the fall of 1927.

The 1926–27 school year brought significant changes to the Berry Schools as junior college courses were added to the curriculum. Although the college classes were taught on the lower campus, this new addition to the school had a direct impact on operations at the mountain campus. In order to accommodate the twenty college students on the lower campus, all first-year high school students were moved to the Foundation School. Additional teachers were added at the Foundation School to accommodate the group

The ruins of Friendship Hall following the fire, 1926.

of freshmen, who were described as "a lively bunch" with a "hardy spirit."[55] Martha Berry's dream of moving her boys' school to the mountain campus was about to be realized, although not at the cost of $1 million as she had earlier projected, and not simply because she thought that the picturesque nature of "Grady and the boys seems to open a generous vein." The move was instead precipitated by the expansion of the school to include first a two-year and then a four-year college. The migration of the boys' school on the lower campus to the Foundation School campus at the foot of Lavender Mountain would necessitate a new curriculum, new buildings and a new name for the operation on the mountain campus. The transition that began in 1926 laid the foundation for dramatic changes in the institution that had begun in a moonshiner's shack only a decade before.

Chapter 3

BERRY'S NEW ERA

*I am more deeply impressed than ever with the far reaching influence of the boys
and girls who leave these Schools.*
—Emily Vanderbilt Hammond

The addition of college courses at the Berry Schools was heralded by
the *Mount Berry News* as "another distinct step forward in education of
those who have to work their way." While more and more of the graduates
of the Berry Schools were going on to attend college, many of them found it
impossible to complete their college-level work because of financial hardships.
Martha Berry envisioned providing the opportunity for men and women with
limited financial means to receive college educations through the same work-
study model that she had developed for younger boys and girls.[56]

The physical plant on the lower campus had expanded considerably since
the early years when the boys lived, worked and studied in wood-frame
buildings on the original eighty-three acres near the Summerville Highway.
The construction in 1915 of the school's first two brick buildings, Blackstone
Hall and the Mount Berry Chapel, established the model for the northward
expansion of the boys' school on the lower campus. By 1926, a quadrangle
framed by brick buildings in the Colonial Revival style had begun to take
shape just north of the original boys' school campus. A new facility for the
girls' school, which had developed about a mile north of the boys' school,
also was under construction at the courtesy of automobile magnate Henry
Ford. A new dormitory and dining hall built of native stone in the Gothic

Revival style were completed on a hilltop across the meadow from the original girls' school campus, and plans were ready for additional buildings in the Ford complex, which would be completed in 1931. The additional buildings on the lower campus, however, would not provide enough room for the rapidly expanding programs at the college level. Although the high school and college women could be accommodated into the foreseeable future in the Ford Buildings, there was not enough room for both the high school boys and the college men on the lower campus.

With the opening of the 1927 school year, the *Mount Berry News* declared, "The Berry Schools entered a new era of service." The school that for the past twenty-five years had been "a shining light in our southland" was about to go "forth into a new sphere of usefulness which is to be even more far-reaching in scope." The college, which had begun the previous year with twenty students, now had over one hundred men and women enrolled. The freshman and sophomore high school boys had been moved to the Foundation School campus, and the name had been changed to the Mount Berry School for Boys (MBSB). The development of the college into a four-year institution by 1930 would necessitate the movement of the remaining high school boys to the mountain campus, and the MBSB would become the base of instruction for all grammar and high school boys.[57]

Almost 700 students were enrolled in the Berry Schools at the opening of the fall term in September 1927. Just over 250 of those students resided on the mountain campus. The boys lived in the newly rebuilt Friendship Hall, Meacham Hall, Pine Lodge and Cherokee Lodge, as well as in two temporary, wood-frame dormitories located between Meacham and Cherokee. Classes were held in the recitation hall, as well as in the new shop building that had been constructed by the boys of native stone the year before. Although isolated from the outside world, the boys on the mountain campus had plenty to keep them busy. Work was nearing completion on the new gymnasium adjacent to the shop and barn complex, and the *Mount Berry News* prodded the MBSB Mountain Lions to "wake up and roar" over this new facility, which ranked among the "best in the state." For the first time, the boys would have an indoor space in which to play basketball and practice gymnastics. Completion of this new facility was eagerly anticipated in February 1928.[58]

The YMCA at the MBSB offered the boys a chance for fellowship while keeping sharp their competitive spirit. Each term, the boys of the individual dormitories competed for the pennant that was awarded to the dormitory with the highest attendance at the "Y" meetings. The boys attended chapel services on Sunday mornings and prayer meetings on Sunday evenings,

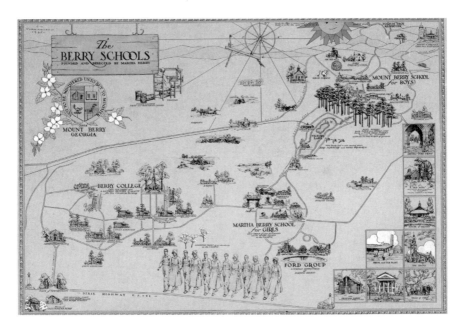

Map of the Berry Schools showing the Mount Berry School for Boys on the mountain campus, 1935.

and the literary societies organized debates, as well as theatrical and musical performances. All the boys attended classes four days a week and worked two days a week to pay their way. They worked in the dining hall preparing and serving food. They worked in the shop making furniture for the dormitories and classrooms. They worked in the barns tending the livestock. They worked in the fields planting and harvesting crops. And they worked on the grounds, carrying out Martha Berry's master plan for the beautification of the campus.

Never one to be satisfied with what nature had wrought, Martha Berry engaged the services of Robert Cridland, a renowned landscape architect from Philadelphia, to prepare landscape designs for the gardens and grounds of her home, Oak Hill, as well as for parts of the school campus. Many of the plans entailed relocating truckloads of holly and rhododendron and assorted shrubberies from the mountain to the area around the buildings and lakes. Students were warned to watch their steps as "those holes you see everywhere on the campus are not to trap the unwary, they are for the many shrubs to be set to ornament our beautiful grounds. Some have thought it a gigantic golf course, and several clumsy folks have taken occasion to fall in them."[59]

An unfinished landscape was not the only peril for the boys at the MBSB. On December 23, 1930, one of the temporary, wood-frame dormitories went up in flames. Almost half of the boys and one faculty member who lived in the dormitory, known as Barracks Two, lost everything they owned. Accommodations for the displaced boys and faculty were made available in the remaining dormitories and in the gymnasium on the mountain campus.[60] Little more than a month later, on January 27, 1930, fire swept through the farm barn and industrial shop buildings adjacent to the gymnasium at the MBSB. The *Mount Berry News* reported that "the refugees of the Barracks Two fire, who were temporarily housed in the gymnasium, narrowly escaped being burned out again. The fire wall between the gym and the barn and the excellent fighting of the fire crew were all that saved the $75,000 gym building." Damage estimates included three trucks, a tractor, twenty tons of hay, two mules and more than $6,000 worth of shop equipment.[61]

The shop and barn were reconstructed during the summer of 1930. The new industrial shop was better equipped than its predecessor, and under the direction of industrial arts teacher George Street, the boys made all the study tables for a new stone dormitory that was also completed during the summer. Known as Pilgrim Hall in honor of the New York friends of Emily Vanderbilt Hammond who made annual pilgrimages to the school, the building housed 125 boys and included "a modern up-to-date dental clinic given by Dr. Proctor," a Boston dentist who had long been a supporter of the school.[62] The Proctor Dental Clinic, staffed by a dental hygienist and Dr. Charles Rounds, provided dental services to all three units of the Berry Schools. By the spring of 1931, Dr. Rounds estimated that the staff of the clinic had carried out over 1,200 cleanings and that he had filled 2,528 teeth. "A good many of the students had never before visited a dentist and many were found who had never owned a tooth-brush," reported Dr. Rounds.[63]

The construction of Pilgrim Hall and the reconstruction of the shop and barn temporarily diverted efforts away from another project on which the boys at the MBSB had been working: the construction of an overshot water mill that could grind corn for the school. The mill, which was completed in the spring of 1931, was alleged to be the third-highest wooden overshot wheel in the country and was considered "an addition to the quaint beauty of the campus."[64]

A visitor to the campus in the fall of 1930, Mrs. Sake Meehan, penned a story for her hometown newspaper in Citronelle, Alabama, that heralded the "natural beauty and healthfulness" of the Berry Schools. But the most significant thing about the school, according to Meehan, was "the persistence of the ideal." In spite of the remarkable growth of the schools from the small log and frame buildings almost thirty years earlier, the character of the schools remained unaltered, wrote Meehan, with all the students neatly attired in their uniforms—overalls and blue shirts for the boys, blue cotton dresses for the girls—and all the students engaged in the work program. Meehan reported that "Mount Berry is now an important educational center. Industrial schools are being founded on its model, and educators from all over the world arrive to study its methods. At Berry the Ideal reigns, but as soundly founded upon and buttressed by the Practical as any institution in the world."[65]

The Berry Ideal, as it was presented to visitors, and the reality, however, did not always align. In 1931, the *Mount Berry News* reported that a study by the psychology class of the high school revealed that the "study habits of the school are poor." Apparently, more time and effort had gone into the work program than into the academic program at the high school, and the boys, who excelled at carrying out their work duties, were proving less industrious when it came to their studies.[66] By August 1933, the boys on the mountain campus began to rebel against the rigors of the work program as well when they staged a brief but widely publicized strike on the mountain campus.

The trouble began when the wages for the boys at the MBSB were cut during the summer of 1933 from sixteen to eighteen cents an hour to ten to twelve cents an hour. Tuition for the year at the MBSB was $150, and many of the students worked full time during the four-month summer break to pay their tuition for the following year. With the reduction in wages, according to Willis Sutton, a student at the MBSB, the boys were no longer able to earn enough money during the summer to cover the cost of their tuition for the year. Sutton and five or six other students organized a strike of the workers at the MBSB on August 28, 1933, to protest the wage cut. The strike, which involved approximately one hundred boys, was short-lived, lasting only a few hours. According to a report in the *New Republic*, school authorities called a general assembly on the mountain campus after the boys failed to show up for work. The faculty and staff were able to persuade the boys to call off the strike, which the boys did after airing their additional grievances and swearing a pledge of loyalty to the Berry Schools.[67] In a letter to Grady Hamrick written several weeks after the strike, Martha Berry expressed concern that "the boys were planning some drastic measures and that they were going to do something to some of the members of the faculty," an indication that she thought the "loyalty oath" sworn by the boys to the school was perhaps less than sincere.[68]

On October 8, 1933, the *Atlanta Constitution* published an extensive article about the strike. Reporter Edwin Holman blamed outside agitators for fomenting the short-lived strike, which he claimed was "frustrated by the students' loyalty." MBSB students had been sent "seditious literature," wrote Holman, which the students promptly turned over to school authorities. The school responded to the attacks by Willis Sutton's cousin Don West and outsiders by publishing a bulletin that recounted how the students had formed a united front against this assault by "outside radical organizations" that sought to "stir up class hatred and prejudice."

According to Robert Alston, chairman of Berry's board of trustees, these "radical organizations" purported to speak for Berry students through the publication of a leaflet that appealed to farmers in Floyd and Bartow County to "rise up in opposition to the school for competing with them in the vegetable and produce markets." According to the leaflet, Berry students were forced to work for low wages, which allowed the school to flood the market with cheap produce and consigned local farmers to a life of poverty, just as it did the students. The leaflets "demanded recognition of students' organizations and representation of the student body" and requested that "students be allowed to investigate the actual cost of maintaining a student and the income derived from the products raised by the students." Other demands included an increase in wages or a decrease in tuition for the students and "that students be allowed to hold two mixed socials every month and get two trips to town each month." Alston stated that a former student was "the brains behind this thing" and reiterated that there had been "no strike and no protest from the students."[69]

Several days later, Berry wrote to her longtime friend and supporter Emily Vanderbilt Hammond with a request that Hammond contact representatives of newspapers "in which the communists who are fighting us say they are going to have published articles that are detrimental to the school."[70] Berry's fear of the "communists" was not unfounded. Don West had helped facilitate the strike among the boys at the MBSB. A former Berry student himself, West had a complicated relationship with the institution. He had been expelled from Berry for leading a boycott of the film *Birth of a Nation* in 1926, yet he had seemingly maintained a good relationship with the school, requesting references and transcripts from President Leland Green shortly after his expulsion.[71] West had achieved some fame in 1932 for the publication of his collection of poems, *Crab Grass*, and he was held up in the March 1932 issue of the *Berry Alumni Quarterly* as embodying "some of Berry's noblest ideals" and as an exemplar of "Berry's golden motto: 'Not to be ministered unto but to minister.'"[72]

The high esteem in which the Berry Schools had held Don West, it seems, was not reciprocated. In addition to assisting his cousin in organizing the August 28 strike, West wrote a letter to the *New Republic* in which he characterized Berry as a "sweatshop" and stated that he thought "the public should be told the nature of this and other missionary institutions with which the South was cursed."[73] West's letter unleashed a flurry of correspondence from supporters of the school, mostly students, as the *New Republic* reported several weeks later. The magazine promised to send an independent investigator to the school to report on the situation.[74]

For a brief period of time, Martha Berry must have feared that her dream had become a nightmare. Both Martha and her school had been blessed by overwhelmingly positive publicity for more than thirty years. Although the school had encountered difficult financial circumstances over the years, including a brief legal dispute related to property taxes and a lawsuit by a student who was injured while working at the school, never before had anyone directly attacked the very foundation of the institution—its work program—in the way that Don West did in the fall of 1933. Although Berry's appeal to Emily Vanderbilt Hammond came too late to stop the publication of Don West's letter in the *New Republic*, Hammond did contact some of her friends in the newspaper business with some success, including Helen Rogers Reid, wife of *Herald Tribune* publisher Ogden Mills Reid. Berry thanked Hammond for her intervention on behalf of the school, noting, "I am sure that it is best for us not to have any more publicity about the 'Communists.'"[75] A week later, Berry reported to Hammond, "We are still getting letters of protest but I feel sure it is best just to ignore them. It was a mistake to pay any attention to them at first, I think. The members of the faculty and all of the students seem united to do anything they can for Berry."[76]

As promised, the *New Republic* sent an investigator to Berry to follow up on the story of the strike. Martha Berry reported to Emily Vanderbilt Hammond that the investigator spent three or four days in Rome, and "we entertained him at the schools one day and did all we could to help the cause." The investigator arrived on site with a list of "disgruntled, former Berry students, which he had secured through Don West, and he went around calling on all of these disgruntled boys," according to Berry. He was given access to the heads of the different departments, as well as the school's books and records, and Martha "entertained him at luncheon," she wrote, adding "we were as nice to him as we could be."[77]

Three months later, the report of the investigator, Hamilton Basso, appeared in the *New Republic*. Basso's report, written in the form of "an open letter to Miss Martha Berry," was a mixed blessing. He was effusive in his praise of the institution, noting that he had "anticipated a few crude buildings off in the hills" but had instead "found dormitories and recitation halls and laboratories that would do credit to a large Eastern university. I was truly astonished," wrote Basso, adding that he could "well understand why you have been called one of the ten greatest women in America and why President Theodore Roosevelt said you were the greatest of them all."[78]

Basso offered what seemed to be a balanced account of the events that had transpired at the MBSB based on his interviews with current faculty, staff and students, as well as with several students who had been expelled in the wake of the strike. While he acknowledged that the school had not treated the boys unfairly, he did raise the issues of too many restrictions and insufficient contact with the outside world as complaints of the boys. The tone of Basso's article, however, hinted at an air of secrecy that pervaded the administration of the school, but his biggest complaint was that he was apparently "trailed" by a detective as if he were a suspicious character during his time in Rome. "Why should I be shadowed," asked Basso, when "there was no conflict between us, no antagonism?" Basso also reported that after returning to New York, he received a letter from one of the students with whom he had spoken while in Rome requesting him not to publish anything that the student had told him when Basso was in Rome. "I have nothing against the Berry Schools and I think it is the greatest school anywhere," wrote the student. "It did great things for me and helped me get a start in life. I am for the School 100 percent." Basso questioned whether the boy had been threatened by school authorities.[79]

Several truths seem to emerge from the events that took place in the later summer and fall of 1933. It seems clear that there was a strike by the boys at the MBSB, even though the strike lasted, at most, a few hours. The precarious financial situation of the institution was also revealed. The cost of operating the Berry Schools the previous year had been over $351,000. The students had paid only slightly more than $27,000 in cash fees during that same period. The balance of the money to operate the school had to be raised by Martha Berry, and in the midst of the Great Depression, raising money to keep schools operating was no easy task. Berry had reduced faculty and staff salaries in an effort to balance the budget and, finally, had resorted to reducing the wages of the students, which resulted in the brief strike on August 28. Martha Berry's influence in curbing what could have been a public relations nightmare was also notable. Although Don West's letter in the *New Republic* did elicit a flurry of letters and led to the more extensive article by Hamilton Basso, the publicity surrounding the labor unrest was, for the most part, favorable toward the institution.

Another truth that was revealed by the events surrounding the strike is the iron fist with which Martha Berry tried to run her institution. Her attempt to isolate the boys on the mountain campus from the outside world and to regulate their lives seemed to be significant factors leading to the work stoppage. The boys wanted more freedom—freedom to visit their families and girlfriends and to smoke. Subsequently, an effort was made to accommodate the boys' requests to permit more interaction with the girls on the lower campus, although such interactions were strictly supervised. Restrictions regarding leaving the campus remained in force, however, as did the prohibition against smoking. Martha Berry remained determined to control her schools and their environment. "She was a detailist," recalled Grady Hamrick's son John, who grew up on the campus, explaining that Berry frequently "wrote letters to my dad about the details."[80] No detail, it seemed, was too small. In preparation for a "sight-seeing trip" for a group of teachers in April 1933, Berry requested that Grady Hamrick "have the sheep, oxen, and all the animals on display" for the visitors.[81] A year later, in April 1934, she instructed Hamrick to make sure that all of the residents of the Possum Trot community and everyone at the MBSB were registered to vote because she wanted to "get a road changed a little later." Berry foresaw that it would be necessary to have the votes of everyone in the Berry community in order to ensure that politicians who favored her cause were elected.[82]

The events of the 1933–34 school year faded into memory, and the MBSB continued to grow with each passing year. In the fall of 1935, the MBSB opened with 319 students—the largest enrollment in its history. A headline in the campus newspaper cried, "'Hang 'Em on Nails' Only Place to Put Students." Pine Lodge, the original log dormitory on the mountain campus, had been damaged by fire earlier in the year, reducing the available dormitory space for the boys. However, the new dairy facility on the mountain campus, which was near completion, included housing for additional students. The dairy was heralded as "one of the most modern in the country," with accommodations in the milking barn for sixty cows and complete facilities and equipment for bottling the milk and making ice cream. All of the dairy operations were moved to the new facility by the summer of 1936. The hog farm was relocated from the college campus to the mountain campus in 1935, and the *Mount Berry News* reported that "the porkers [were] now enjoying their new home."[83]

Like all of the other buildings on the mountain campus, the new dairy was constructed by the boys. The dairy, built between 1931 and 1937, served as a training facility where the boys were taught the basics of bricklaying. Gordon Keown recalled that "the dairy building is just a homemade proposition, and we didn't hurry about it. It was done over a period of five or six years, but instead of letting the brick classes practice putting up walls and then tearing them down, we'd build a permanent building. We made that one building at a time. We'd make the brick, and then the boys in the bricklaying classes would lay up the walls. Maybe the wall of a certain building would stand there a year before we could get out in the woods and cut the trees. We sawed the lumber on our own sawmills for rafters, etc."[84]

Another construction project on the mountain campus during this period was Frost Chapel. Money for the chapel was given by Mr. and Mrs. Howard Frost of Los Angeles, who visited the school in 1935. Howard Frost had made a fortune running the Los Angeles Pressed Brick Company, which he had inherited from his father. The Frosts were impressed with the religious life at Berry and decided to build a chapel on the mountain campus in honor of their son, John Laurance Frost, who had died the year before. John Frost had been an active member of the YMCA and participated in Christian outreach while enrolled at Stanford University, and his parents believed that construction of the chapel at the MBSB would "bring the inspiring influence of their son's life in a widening circle."[85] The boys on the mountain campus worked feverishly to complete installation of the pews in the chapel before the October 14 dedication ceremony.

Just two years after they completed work on Frost Chapel, the boys began construction of a new library facility at the MBSB. Paid for by the family of George Barstow III, the new library was designed by New York architect Stuart Turner and built of native fieldstone. Barstow, a twenty-one-year-old student at Julliard, had perished along with adventurer Richard Halliburton and other members of Halliburton's crew while crossing the Pacific Ocean in a Chinese junk known as the *Sea Dragon* in 1939. Barstow was remembered as a "handsome young man deeply interested in music and literary work," so it seemed appropriate to his family that a library be built in his name. The new building, Barstow Library, was dedicated on October 26, 1940.[86]

Opposite, top: Boys building the Normandy dairy barns, circa 1928.

Opposite, bottom: Boys milking in the new dairy, circa 1934.

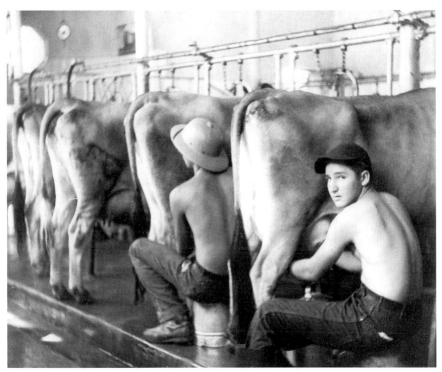

As the nation emerged from the Great Depression into the cauldron of war in 1941, the campus spirit at Berry was unusually somber. President Franklin Roosevelt's request for a declaration of war in December 1941 cast a pall across the campus, but it also inspired new patriotism in the boys at the MBSB. However, a dark cloud loomed over the campus. Martha Berry had been transported to Saint Joseph's Hospital in Atlanta in September 1941 to receive treatment for numerous health problems. In a report to the board of trustees in late 1941, Dr. Leland Green wrote, "The country's peril and Miss Berry's illness seem to constitute a challenge for a double portion of loyalty and sacrifice."[87] By year's end, it seemed apparent that Martha Berry would not recover from her illness. She died on Friday, February 27, 1942, at Saint Joseph's Hospital, and her body was brought back to the campus the next day. All work ceased on the campus on Saturday, February 28, and the students somberly lined the road from the main entrance gate to Barnwell Chapel for the arrival of Martha Berry's body, which lay in state until her funeral on Sunday afternoon.[88] The death of the founder meant the end of an era for the Berry Schools.

Chapter 4

YEARS OF GRACE

The responsibility for carrying forward the labors of Miss Berry is a challenge to tax the ability and energy of the best.
—*Philip Weltner*

The death of Martha Berry was a tremendous blow to the Berry Schools. She had been not only the spiritual leader of the institution but also the principal fundraiser. In her "last letter" to the board of trustees, written on July 1, 1925, Berry implored the trustees to "carry on the work in the spirit in which it was founded, keeping it always within the means of poor boys and girls; maintaining the industrial work and teaching the dignity of labor." To the alumni, Berry also wrote a last letter dated July 1, 1925, in which she entreated the alumni to "use all of your influence to hold the Schools to the original plan: simple living, work, prayer, the Bible being taught, Christian teachers, keeping the Schools a separate community, protecting and guarding the property and the good name of the Schools." Berry's letter to the alumni concluded with her prayer that "the Schools may stand through the ages, for the honor and glory of God and for the Christian training of poor boys and girls of the mountains and country districts."[89]

The world in which the board of trustees found itself in 1942 was vastly different from the world in which Martha Berry lived at the time she had written the letter almost two decades earlier. The world was at war, enrollment at the school for young men had stagnated, a new income tax structure had negatively affected contributions to the school and the public school system in Georgia had expanded. Perhaps just as significantly, the Berry Schools had changed rather dramatically in those seventeen years between 1925 and 1942. The school now included a four-year college that eclipsed the high schools in enrollment. Total enrollment in the college had surpassed that of the high schools in 1940, when the college boasted 677 students. The enrollment in the boys' high school was 380 and in the girls' high school, 126. At the time of Martha Berry's death in 1942, the college had 678 students enrolled while the boys' high school had declined to 338. The girls' high school boasted a slight increase to 138.[90] The numbers, however, do not tell the whole story of the monumental shift that had taken place between 1925 and 1942. The boys' school, which was Martha Berry's first boarding school and a sentimental favorite among the alumni and friends of Berry, had been relocated from its original campus to the mountain campus. The Farm School that had been created in 1916 and its successor on the mountain campus, the Foundation School, had both been phased out as the mountain campus operation was modified to accommodate the high school boys. Always pragmatic, Martha Berry had not shied away from modifying her schools in response to societal changes while reaffirming her commitment to the principles on which she had founded the institution: education of the head, the heart and the hands.

As part of a planning process, the board, under the leadership of John A. Sibley, engaged the services of Victor Butterfield of Wesleyan University in Connecticut to conduct a study of the schools and make recommendations regarding the present and future operations of the institution. Butterfield's report, submitted to Sibley on April 28, 1942, hailed the "amazingly contagious" spirit of Martha Berry and the resulting "deep spiritual vitality" of the schools as the institution's greatest strength. Berry students seemed to "relish their work and find a genuine dignity in every task, no matter how menial." The students also seemed "exceedingly anxious to learn" and had "a nice sense of service," according to Butterfield.[91] Faculty morale, on the other hand, left something to be desired. Salaries were "discouragingly low," there was no retirement program and many of the faculty felt that "the administration acts secretly and by means of grapevine information and without frank and open dealings."[92]

Butterfield observed that the work program was "first rate," but the academic program was in need of great help. He opined that "Miss Berry apparently tended to minimize the importance of training the mind, largely, I think because she was so fearful of such training in isolation from the practical problems and the real life of students."[93] The work program had

Boys in the auditorium of the Mount Berry School for Boys Recitation Hall, circa 1939.

long overshadowed the academic program at Berry, and Butterfield would not be the first or the last outsider to make such an observation. Butterfield expressed concern that student and faculty turnover at the MBSB was "far out of proportion to what it should be" and added that "there was some feeling expressed at the college that the high school was becoming a kind of reform school for incorrigibles, that because of the competition of the consolidated public high schools, the only boys who were sent to the Berry high school were those whom parents would not put up with."[94]

The schools were in desperate need of "a very rare leadership," noted Butterfield, and "there is no person or persons in the present scene who can really carry on in terms of the long future." Butterfield felt that the "possibility of the Berry Schools for the future [was] perfectly immense," but much depended on the board's finding an outstanding leader for the institution. "If the Schools should continue to be what they now are they would more than justify their existence," wrote Butterfield, "but there is a certain psychological danger in trying to stay the same. Under such circumstances an institution is apt to get literal minded, pedantic, and petty, and to lose sight of the spirit behind the form."[95]

John Sibley and the board of trustees took Butterfield's report to heart and began an aggressive search for "a very rare" leader who could shepherd the schools into the second half of the twentieth century. Sibley thought he had found the perfect candidate in Philip Weltner, an Atlanta attorney who had served as a chancellor of the University of Georgia and had extensive administrative, business and educational experience. Weltner was considered to be a turnaround artist, having taken charge of several businesses that were not doing well and putting them "on a sound basis." Weltner was offered the job of director at Berry by Sibley in June 1943, and although he was "profoundly grateful" for the offer, he felt compelled to decline. The "immediate problem," observed Weltner, "comes down to whether or not a man almost 56, yet active, inquiring, and impatient, who is essentially an innovator can at that age fit into an institution which in some respects is almost a shrine, and not fall foul of resentments, the normal reaction to his daring, which in the end would defeat his most devoted efforts. My conclusion is that the chance of such a frustration is only too probable."[96] Weltner foresaw the difficulties that anyone would encounter in succeeding such a revered leader as Martha Berry, especially someone who was truly innovative and forward thinking.

Although he declined to assume a full-time leadership position at Berry, Weltner did agree to join the board of trustees. He was named vice chairman of the board and appointed to the executive committee, and he agreed to serve temporarily in an "advisory capacity" for the school. Sibley envisioned Weltner's rendering two important services to the Berry Schools: strengthening the present administrative setup and helping locate a suitable permanent leader for the institution.[97] Board member Lamar Westcott, in a letter to chairman Sibley, noted that "there are definitely some administrative matters which need adjusting," and he agreed that Weltner seemed like the right man for the job.[98] Westcott was concerned that everyone at Berry be informed that Weltner had "the authority from the board of trustees to do whatever is necessary to straighten out matters at the school." Rumors that "discipline among the students was very lax" were circulating, reported Westcott; and he reminded Sibley that at the last board meeting, a staff member reported that "certain students were refusing to wear the adopted uniform of the school in defiance of the rules." Westcott felt that the current leadership at the school was not as strong as it should be, and he hoped that Weltner would help "to correct these conditions regardless of who [sic] it might affect. If students do not want to abide by the rules in wearing the adopted uniform of the school," continued Westcott, "they should be dismissed without any hesitance whatever, and if there are any other persons connected with the school who are failing to do their duty for any reason whatsoever, they should be dismissed. I feel that it is time for a thorough cleanup and reorganization."[99]

Empowered by the board of trustees, Weltner arrived on campus in late July 1943 and began a systematic review of the schools' operations. "I believe the school business is similar to any other," wrote Weltner to Gordon Keown, acting director. "In manufacturing, the job is to locate and remove bottlenecks whether in sales or production, management or finances. Schools, to my way of thinking, are no different. With us the problems turn around such matters as dormitory space, classroom facilities, the teaching staff, etc." Addressing the issue of the student-work program, Weltner stated that "the work at which we put our students should be so necessary that if students were not employed to do it we would have to get outside help for that purpose."[100] Weltner wanted a complete accounting of the work that needed to be done and the number of students and staff available to do it. The impact of World War II was being felt throughout the institution as enrollment, especially for male students, decreased significantly. Acting director Gordon Keown reported to Weltner that the "labor situation is growing more and more acute," and his "chief concern at the moment is how we are to meet our daily problems." At the height of harvest season, the school did not have enough male students to harvest the crops or milk the cows and was "compelled to use girls more generally in the industrial work."[101]

By October 1943, Weltner had completed his assessment of the Berry Schools and prepared a report for the board of trustees. Sibley and other members of the board had continued to hope that Weltner would reconsider his objection to assuming a full-time leadership position at the school, but in his cover letter to the assessment report, he reiterated his unwillingness to take on a more permanent role. While "the invitation to become head of Berry is a great honor," he wrote, "the responsibility for carrying forward the labors of Miss Berry is a challenge to tax the ability and energy of the best." Weltner feared that "Berry's staunchest friends may come to regard me as an iconoclast" if he were put in charge of the institution. His attached report, he explained, avoided no issue, withheld nothing and glossed over nothing; and he felt sure that after the board members studied the report, they would agree with him that the leadership of Berry "should be committed to other hands."[102]

Weltner's report offered an unvarnished look at Berry that was no doubt hard for many members of the institution's leadership to swallow, but it was also sorely needed. "Berry's aim had always been superb; its reach had fallen short of that aim," wrote Weltner, adding that the school had not "kept abreast of the rising tide of educational opportunity." According to Weltner, the long-term success of Berry would depend on the strength of its educational program, and the program at present was far from outstanding. The quality of the faculty needed great improvement; otherwise, "the students who continue coming to Berry will be merely the culls, coming to us because they are unable to go elsewhere." The war years that had caused for Berry so many difficulties, Weltner suggested, "may become...veritable 'years of grace'" during which time the school could reinvent itself in a way that would ensure its success well into the future.[103] The organization had been built around Martha Berry, stated Weltner, and "most people familiar with the Berry Schools today will admit that these arrangements were feasible only because Miss Berry had the capacity to make them work. You should be told flatly that with Miss Berry away from the helm, the organization as she built it is 'gone with the wind.'"[104]

Weltner proposed that the director's position be eliminated, explaining that it was a position "rarely employed in educational circles." Martha Berry had adopted the title of director of the schools, but as Weltner pointed out, she was "so intimately associated in the public mind with the institution which she founded that whatever title she selected for herself was of little consequence." At most educational institutions, the president was the person responsible for the public contacts and internal control, and so should it be at Berry. Weltner also suggested that the school begin preparing an annual operations budget, which he claimed was an innovation for Berry. He reported that he was told at least a dozen times that "Miss Berry never had a budget. When she needed money, she went out and got it." Weltner did not doubt that this was so, but he noted "what was possible for Miss Martha, may be folly for others to imitate."[105]

A disconnect existed between the academic program and the work program, reported Weltner, and it was "not uncommon for a teacher to advise this and for a foreman to direct that." Work supervisors had "no conception of what the boys have been taught," a disconnect that led to conflicts and confusion for the students. The academic programs at both the college and high school levels needed a complete overhaul, and the work program should serve to reinforce what the students were learning in the classroom.[106] The dramatic decline in enrollment from 1940 to 1943 (the college had declined from 648 to 305 and the MBSB from 359 to 149) could be attributed to a combination of the ongoing war, as well as to Berry's failure to conduct a "concerted drive to attract students who need Berry and whom Berry needs."[107] Weltner recommended phasing out the high schools, both boys and girls, by omitting the freshman high school classes in 1944 and discontinuing the sophomore classes the next year.[108]

Berry was no longer the only option in the area for poor boys and girls. The Floyd County Board of Education had consolidated several small schools in the area into one complete unit, opening the Armuchee High School in 1941.[109] In light of the changing landscape of public education, Weltner felt that more resources should be directed toward improving the academic program of the college. Regarding personnel, Weltner suggested that the school needed to rid itself of many of its current staff, whom he claimed had once served their purpose but were now an encumbrance on the institution. Weltner acknowledged that his recommendations would be controversial, noting that "perhaps the hardest test of all will come in facing the criticism of alumni, friends of discharged employees, and worst of all, the possible displeasure of old friends of Miss Martha Berry, who in the past have liberally given of their means. Time and again it will be dinned into your ears; 'This is not the way Miss Berry would have wanted it.'" While admitting that "there may be some ground for such a charge," Weltner offered that the standard by which to judge the proposed changes was "one which Miss Martha would have approved—'Sacrifice every interest; yes, if need be, my very memory, if such sacrifice is for our boys and girls—better it is to minister than to be ministered unto.'"[110]

The Weltner Report, while controversial and divisive, offered many useful recommendations for the foundering institution. John Sibley described the report as "very thorough and enlightening," adding, "In striving for new goals and making necessary adaptations, we must not lose the beauty and charm of the place nor the deep spiritual feeling that has made Berry unique."[111] Board member G. Lister Carlisle proclaimed that "the report is very important. Its approach is able, direct and cold blooded," and while he was in agreement with Weltner's overall recommendation that the educational program must be strengthened, he could not yet accept all of the proposed changes, which he described as "drastic."[112] Over the next several decades, many of Weltner's recommendations would be adopted, although he did not personally implement them. He continued to serve on Berry's board of trustees, even after he was named president of Oglethorpe University in Atlanta in 1944. Weltner's warning about the "hardest test" being that of facing the criticism of alumni and friends proved to be prophetic.

Although Weltner's recommendation to begin phasing out the MBSB was not followed, the Martha Berry School for Girls was discontinued in the 1950s. A phased approach was used between 1953 and 1956, when the last group of girls graduated. Many of Weltner's recommendations regarding leadership changes were carried out. Among the changes was the departure of Grady Hamrick from his position as principal of the Mount Berry School for Boys in 1945. Hamrick's leaving was mourned by the boys of the MBSB. He was a father figure to the boys, and he had served as the head of the various schools at the mountain campus since 1916. Hamrick had been instrumental in the development of the MBSB. He and the boys had constructed all the buildings that composed the MBSB, and he had overseen both the work and academic programs. Ralph McDonald (46H) admired Hamrick greatly and remembered him as a good disciplinarian who was able to make the boys feel at home.[113] Bennie Shipp (47H) credited Hamrick with being the most influential person of his high school years, recalling that Hamrick was strict but had "a loving heart."[114]

Hamrick's dismissal caused great sadness among the boys at the MBSB, but the board of trustees had begun to pursue a course of action designed to increase the academic rigor of the institution. Although Hamrick was a graduate of the Berry School and had furthered his education at the Berry Junior College and with additional studies at the University of Georgia and the University of North Carolina, he did not have a bachelor's degree. What had been considered an acceptable level of education for the head of the boys' school in the 1910s and 1920s was considered no longer adequate by the 1940s. Following his departure from Berry, Hamrick and his wife, Ethel, moved to Macon, Georgia, where he served as superintendent of the Masonic Children's Home of Georgia. Hamrick's dismissal represented a shift in the mode of operation at the Berry Schools.

Following Hamrick's departure, James Armour Lindsay, head of the education department at the college, assumed the job of MBSB principal on an interim basis. When Lindsay was offered the position of president of the Berry Schools in 1946, he was succeeded by Kenneth Moore, who remained at the school for only a year before assistant principal Fred Loveday, a Berry College alumnus, was named principal of the MBSB. According to MBSB alumnus Bob Kayler (59H), Loveday, who would head the MBSB for two decades, had a "remarkable understanding of the adolescent mind."[115] Bill Segrest (48H) recalled that "you didn't get away with anything with Mr. Loveday, but he wasn't a tyrant. I think he respected that we were kids in high school." Segrest recounted an episode when he and three of his classmates sneaked off the campus to see some girls in Rockmart near the end of his senior year. As Segrest and his accomplices crept back into the dorm under cover of darkness, they were surprised to see Loveday's cigar glowing in the dark hallway. "All right, I'll see you in the morning," said Loveday sternly. The next day, the boys reported to Loveday's office as requested. "I'm going

Principal Fred Loveday and students in front of the dining hall, 1958.

to have to think about this—you're due to graduate in a couple of weeks," said Loveday to the boys who were trembling in fear. "There was a real question in my mind if I was going to graduate," Segrest remembered, adding, "Mr. Loveday let us stew until about three days before graduation" before letting the boys off the hook.[116]

"It was as if he had eyes in the back of his head," remembered Don Fite (51H), who described Loveday as "not strong and forceful, but wily." Fite recalled how Loveday would stand up in the dining hall during lunch and announce, "There's been a problem developed, and I need to talk to some of you in my office after lunch. You know who you are." Inevitably, one or two boys would show up to confess transgressions of which Loveday was not even aware, but the principal never tipped his hand. More than anything, the boys did not want to disappoint Loveday, and they would rather go to him and confess their sins than have him hunt them down. "Fred Loveday was the most influential person in my life," stated Fite, a sentiment echoed by many of the boys who attended the MBSB during Loveday's tenure.[117]

Nearly all of the boys who attended the boys' high school between 1947 and 1966, when Loveday departed, had an experience in which they were outwitted and outmaneuvered by Loveday. According to Bob Kayler, Loveday "had an immense capacity for tolerating outrageous behavior, leaving the final outcomes of the boys' lives in the hands of God, while providing the counsel and direction that any good father would to his own children." Kayler recalled that he "had the opportunity to receive [Loveday's] guidance" on many occasions, citing what he referred to as the "floor wax" incident as being the "most significant in my life." It was, Kayler noted, a fine example of Loveday's "sixth sense" and "how [someone] could be in so many places at once and seemingly know every bit of mischief boys could create." It was during his sophomore year that Kayler and several of his classmates discovered a batch of "home brew" hidden in a stump hole near Pilgrim Hall. After sneaking the jug back into the dormitory, Kayler and his friends could not resist the temptation to taste the concoction, which "looked awful and tasted worse," recalled Kayler. Surmising that the fermentation process was not quite complete, Kayler stashed the jug in his closet and covered it with a towel.

A week later, Kayler was summoned from his English class by Loveday, who stated that the dorm mother, Mrs. Winton, had discovered a "strange concoction" in Kayler's closet. "Yes, sir," replied Kayler, "it is floor wax," adding that he had made it using a recipe from his mother. "If I call your mother, she will tell me she sent you this recipe?" inquired Loveday as he and Kayler arrived at the dormitory. "Yes, sir," replied Kayler, knowing that he needed to get in touch with his mother quickly to warn her that Loveday might call. Loveday inquired about the ingredients in this homemade floor wax, and Kayler reeled off a list of likely ingredients including "corn meal, molasses, carbonated water and yeast." When Loveday questioned the wisdom of including molasses in floor wax, Kayler offered that the yeast "attacks the sugar in the molasses and makes an alcohol base that cuts the stickiness out." Loveday gave Kayler an opportunity to demonstrate the effectiveness of this magic brew on the floor of Kayler's dorm room and observed that, rather than providing a sheen to the floor, Kayler's special mix merely made it sticky. Kayler explained that the mix was not yet ready. "All right," said Loveday, "put the cover back on the jug and place it in the box. Let's get you back to class, and I want to see you at nine o'clock tomorrow morning in my office." He added, "I think I'll call your mother to get the particulars on this wax."

Kayler dashed back to the dorm immediately after class and tried in vain to call his mother, who was out of town visiting relatives. Following a long, fretful night, Kayler realized that he needed to come clean with Loveday. Summoning all of his courage, Kayler reported to the principal's office early the next morning and confessed that the liquid was home brew, not floor wax, but that he had not made it. "Yes, I know all about it," Loveday replied and proceeded to tell Kayler "who made it, where, when and how, including the real ingredients. He then told me who was with me when we took the stuff from the stump hole, that we had tasted it, and that we were saving it for the holidays," added Kayler, although "he did not tell me how he had come by all this information." Loveday gave Kayler a "stern lecture about the evils of alcohol and how we might have poisoned ourselves playing around with something the dangers of which we had no idea" and announced, "I'll let you know how much you have to dig."

At the time, boys who got into trouble were given the task of digging out tree stumps for removal so that new trees could be planted. Kayler figured he deserved many hours of such hard labor, but it was two weeks before he received a small postcard from the principal in his mailbox. Attached to the card was "a small bronze plaque with the Lord's Prayer printed on it" and in the corner, in the tiniest letters Kayler had ever seen, were the initials "F.H.L." Loveday never mentioned the floor wax incident or digging to Kayler again. "Apparently, he figured I had taken my lesson to heart and that further punishment would serve little purpose," surmised Kayler, adding, "He was right! I know I deserved to have to dig long and hard, but he was willing to let the lesson stand and leave the rest to God and me." At his class reunion in 2009, Kayler reported that he kept that little plaque in his Bible to this day as a reminder that Loveday "trusted me to find the right path for my life."[118]

The annals of MBSB history are filled with similar stories of Loveday's firm hand but light touch. He won the hearts and minds of the boys who were under his charge, and in the words of high school alumnus Tom Butler (65A), Loveday "orchestrated a cast of characters" to create an "intangible magic" at the school on the mountain campus. The problems encountered by Loveday at the boys' school went well beyond adolescent mischief, however. The boys awoke at 3:00 a.m. on the morning of November 27, 1955, to discover the Recitation Hall engulfed in flames. In spite of the valiant efforts of the students to fight the fire, according to the *Mount Berry News*, "all but the thick stone walls and part of the wing nearest Barstow Library" were destroyed. The students did manage to save a few desks and some laboratory equipment. The loss was estimated at $150,000. In the wake of the fire, students and staff all pitched in to set up classrooms in the shop and gymnasium building, and the MBSB "continued classes without having to lose a period."

Three weeks after the fire, Loveday reported that he had received many gifts from students and alumni for the reconstruction of the Recitation Hall.[119] Clearing of the rubble from the site began immediately, and the school hired J.P. Roberts Construction Company to reconstruct the Recitation Hall. The new building, which was paid for by a combination of insurance money and gifts from donors, was completed little more than a year after the fire; and on December 3, 1956, classes were held in the new Recitation Hall.[120]

Another disaster occurred on September 2, 1957, when a storage barn at the dairy caught fire. The barn, which contained hay and wood shavings for the cattle barns across the green, burned rapidly. The boys of the MBSB assisted three Rome fire companies in combating the blaze for more than four hours, but the damage was extensive, estimated at more than $60,000.[121]

The fires that plagued the Berry Schools, while devastating, were likely less traumatic for Loveday than the leadership turmoil that the institution experienced between 1944 and 1956. The death of the founder in 1942, followed by the retirement of longtime president Leland Green in 1944, sent the school into a difficult period during which the institution had six presidents in just over a decade. As Philip Weltner had predicted, many members of the faculty and staff held fast to what they believed to be the wishes of Martha Berry, as expressed in her "last letter" from 1925, and

Students fighting the fire at the Normandy barns, 1957.

believed that the schools should remain an isolated community with a focus on educating the rural poor. However, improvements in the public school system, demographic changes wrought by World War II and the Servicemen's Readjustment Act of 1944 combined to make Berry's original educational model obsolete. The school had changed since 1925, and much of that change had been at the behest of Martha Berry herself. But more than a decade after her death, the school was at a crossroads. Enrollment was down, and the institution's financial situation was precarious. The "years of grace," as Philip Weltner had called this turbulent period, came to a close with the arrival of a new president, Dr. John R. Bertrand, in the summer of 1956. Bertrand would oversee the difficult transition into the second half of the twentieth century and would remain at the helm until 1979. As Weltner had predicted, the decades ahead would bring many changes to all of the units of the institution, including the MBSB.

Chapter 5

WHAT WOULD MARTHA BERRY DO?

Miss Berry and her coworkers never rested on their laurels because—always—
there were changing needs, new courageous and ingenious approaches by which to
get the job done.
—John R. Bertrand

John Bertrand arrived at the Berry Schools from the University of Nevada, where he had served as the dean and director of the Fleischmann College of Agriculture and Home Economics. He was well aware that he was stepping into a volatile situation at Berry. He had been warned by board chairman William McChesney Martin of the internal ideological struggle that was ongoing at Berry between the traditionalists, who wanted to adhere strictly to the ideas set forth in Martha Berry's 1925 letters, and the progressives, who favored a more dynamic approach for the institution. Recalibrating the role of the work program and achieving accreditation for the college were two important issues that Martin and other members of the Berry community, including many students, believed were critical to the survival of the school.

Bertrand brought to Berry a great appreciation for the institution's history and tradition but also a vision for the future. At the opening faculty convocation for the 1956–57 school year, with a nod to the past but an eye clearly on the future, Bertrand challenged the faculty to join him in the effort to improve the "effectiveness" of the schools. "Unless we are to fail Miss Berry, unless we are to fail the many dedicated persons who have served

Dr. and Mrs. Bertrand and family, circa 1956.

this institution, unless we are to fail the eternal principles upon which the schools were founded, it is our collective responsibility to see that this great institution continues to grow in effectiveness—yes, surpass even its founder's accomplishments," stated Bertrand. "It will be to the everlasting credit of Martha Berry, her generosity, her faith, and her genius if those of us here now have the courage to dream new dreams, conceive new methods, and take new bold action based on the highest intelligence available to use in this second half of the 20th century," he continued. Giving a hint of the vision that he had for the future, Bertrand observed that "in a single decade, Berry's role has ceased to be solely that of a champion of young men and young women of the rural South who have limited means. It must now compete in a distinctive way with other great institutions of higher learning in the South and in the United States."[122]

Bertrand's opening remarks at his first faculty convocation made clear to the Berry community that the days of looking backward for all the answers to the schools' problems were over. Little more than a year later, Bertrand was able to report that the "long-held objective" of obtaining accreditation from the Southern Association of Colleges and Schools for Berry College had been achieved. In announcing this achievement, Bertrand stated, "We need to preserve and strengthen the fundamental values of this institution;

but we cannot afford to cling needlessly to traditions no longer relevant, to objectives no longer valid, to methods no longer applicable, or to hopes no longer realistic."[123]

After receiving permission from the board of trustees, Bertrand appointed an Educational Advisory Committee to carry out what was described as a "thorough and comprehensive re-appraisal" of the schools' operations.[124] The thirteen-member committee was chaired by the director of college and university administration of the U.S. Office of Education, Ernest V. Hollis, and included two Berry alumni and Berry's dean emeritus, S.H. Cook. The school faced "at least two crucial problems. The first was educational; the second was financial," according to the committee. Throughout 1957, "central in the thinking of the Educational Advisory Committee was this question: what would Martha Berry do if she were alive today?" Unanimously, the committee agreed: "She would not adopt a do-nothing policy no matter what the situation was."[125]

The Executive Summary of the Educational Advisory Committee's report distilled the "two crucial problems" into six "plain facts" as follows:

1. *Since 1942 the educational objectives have become blurred; some academic activities have over-expanded; some have proliferated.*
2. *The academic ability of many students is below par.*
3. *The salaries of the faculty and staff members are shockingly low.*
4. *The industrial enterprises as a whole are losing money.*
5. *The auxiliary enterprises are not self-sustaining.*
6. *The work program—though sound in principle—has gotten out of hand.*[126]

The time had come for the Berry Schools to make significant changes in its programs and mode of operation. "Neither rural nor urban life today is what it was in 1902 or 1942," wrote committee member Laurence Campbell, and the Berry Schools should not shy away from embracing change. "If she had not believed in change," noted Campbell, "Martha Berry would never have founded her schools." According to Campbell, "Martha Berry understood the difference between changing basic principles and changing the application of the principles." Now was a time to change the application of Martha Berry's principles while adhering to the three major objectives of education at the Berry Schools: educating the head, the heart and the hands.[127]

Although the bulk of the Educational Survey report focused on the college and overall administrative operations, a separate section addressed the MBSB. Noting that the "aims and ideals of the Mount Berry School for

Boys and Berry College basically are the same," the report added that the MBSB was "on the one hand unique and distinctive yet on the other hand is an integral part of The Berry Schools."[128] By this time, the MBSB offered two programs for high school boys: an academic program for boys who planned to enter college and a "general" program for those who did not have college aspirations. According to the study, the school still offered a robust selection of courses in agriculture, even though the principal of the school reported that demand for instruction in agriculture was on the decline.[129] Missing from the curriculum were courses in choral music, orchestra, fine arts, typewriting, bookkeeping and other related commercial subjects—all subjects that were being taught at "good public high schools" at the time.[130]

In 1958 the MBSB had a total enrollment of 205, with 12 of those considered full-time work students. Enrollment had declined significantly since the 1930s, when the MBSB routinely claimed more than 300 total students. The small class size at the MBSB, with an average around 20, was laudable because the individual attention afforded each student often made up for the lack of the most current technologies or modern teaching techniques. Of great concern, however, was the fact that the work schedule took precedence over the academic schedule. Each student worked a full day two days a week and attended classes four days a week. Student work schedules were decided by class—freshmen worked Friday and Saturday and attended classes on Monday through Thursday, sophomores worked Monday and Tuesday and attended classes on Wednesday through Saturday and so on. Since the classes met only four days a week, each class period was longer than in the public high schools.

Committee members questioned whether it was reasonable to expect students at the MBSB "to do in four days work which public high school students have five days to do." The work program also limited the number of extracurricular activities for the boys, according to the committee. Other constraints on extracurricular activities included a shortage of "qualified teachers to carry on these activities on top of full class loads and dormitory duties" and a shortage of funds. The boys' social life was also severely limited because there were no longer any high school girls on the Berry campus with whom to arrange such activities as parties and dances.[131] Although few of the MBSB alumni from this period complained about the work program's consuming too much of their time, the absence of social activities with girls was a recurring complaint, especially after the closing of the Martha Berry School for Girls in 1956.

Of great concern for the future of the MBSB was the fact that there was "no sustained or organized program of recruitment" for the school. There

The Gate of Opportunity reflecting the names of the two remaining schools, 1963.

was no systematic effort made to "attract boys who need the program because of any of its notable aspects—academic, religious, work or other." Word of mouth appeared to be the principal method by which potential students learned about the school, and the vetting process for new students seemed to be based on whether the school had a vacancy. The official requirements for admission, as stated in the Berry Schools *Bulletin*, were that the boy be fourteen years old, have completed the eighth grade, agree to comply with the regulations of the school and be approved by the principal and the registrar. Preference was given to "applicants from rural areas in Georgia and neighboring Southern states," and applicants were expected to "present satisfactory evidence of good moral character, normal mental ability, and physical soundness." Other considerations for admission specified that a potential student have "(1) a definite financial hardship, (2) an earnestness of purpose, (3) a willingness to work, and (4) a capacity for both academic and spiritual growth."[132] For the principal and registrar at the MBSB, financial hardship seemed to be the most important factor when evaluating a boy for admission to the high school.

Changes in public education in Georgia were perhaps the greatest threat to the MBSB. In 1902, the state had only five public high schools. Indeed, Martha Berry began her school after recognizing that young boys in the mountains of northwest Georgia had no access to public education. By mid-century, nearly all the boys enrolled at the MBSB lived within ten miles of a public high school when they were at home.[133] No longer could the school count on the lack of education alternatives to fill its roster. Whereas most students in the early decades of the school came because they had no schools nearby, now students were more likely to come because of problems at home. Fewer than half of the boys at the MBSB came from homes where both parents were together, and 45 percent came from families with four or more children.[134]

Some of the boys had no living parents, like Art Pugh (52H), who was orphaned at four months of age. Pugh's mother died three weeks after he was born, and his father died a few months later in a coal-mining accident. Pugh and his brother Luther (51H) were homeless when they made their way to the MBSB. "Berry was the first real home I ever had," recalled Pugh, adding, "I thought I'd died and gone to heaven when I got here."[135] Frank Adams (54H), who came to Berry from Lee County in southwest Georgia, recalled that, although there were public schools in the area, they were not very good. But the main reason he left home was that the house was too crowded. Frank was the oldest of seven children, and he had no privacy, he remembered, adding that "living conditions were so crowded that I had to sleep in the same bed with my brothers."[136]

Pugh and Adams perhaps represented extreme cases of hardship at the MBSB, but their stories were not atypical. Many boys reported that they came from broken homes or that one of their parents was no longer living, but in contrast to the student body of the school's early years, most of the boys did not come from farms or rural homes in the mountains. Perhaps more importantly, most of the boys did not express a vocational interest in agriculture or industrial arts.[137] The demographics of the school had changed dramatically, but the academic and work programs remained much the same as they had been during Martha Berry's lifetime. The MBSB, while a refuge for many of the boys who lived there, was on the cusp of becoming academically irrelevant.

The 1913 amendment to the schools' early charter stated that the mission was "to carry on a school to meet the needs of poor boys and girls alike, from the rural districts." At that time, many of the graduates of the Berry Schools returned to the rural areas from which they had come and worked in agriculture. In what seems almost prescient, Martha Berry amended the charter again in 1931, not only to include an offering of college work without specifying restrictions on the background of the students, but also to broaden the base for students below the college level to include not just "mountain boys and girls" but also "boys and girls and young men and young women from other locations."[138] The wholesale migration from farm to factory that characterized the first half of the twentieth century was barely a recognizable trend in northwest Georgia when Berry broadened the parameters for the student body at her schools.

John Bertrand was keenly aware that alluding to the actions Martha Berry had taken in the past to ensure that her schools remained relevant would help gain acceptance for proposed changes in the future. He cited actions taken by the founder, such as the charter amendments, in his summation of the situation at Berry that was incorporated into the 1958 consultants' report. Although Bertrand believed that the future for the Berry Schools was promising, he also issued a warning that "Berry will falter irreparably if its program continues to be built on the assumption that the students who enroll with us cannot attend elsewhere, since opportunities for the economically handicapped are available today in almost every educational institution." The role that Bertrand envisioned Berry serving was "in its continuing to provide for deserving young people a distinctive educational offering which combines the academic, the work, and the religious aspects of the program for which Berry has been noted for more than half a century." The institution should also adopt a plan that made it possible "for parents and students to pay in accord with their means a larger share of the cost of the distinctive educational opportunity which Berry offers."[139]

The 1958 consultants' report revealed an institution at a crossroads. The schools were operating at a significant deficit, and in May 1957, the board had approved the transfer of $400,000 from reserves to cover operating expenses for the next two years.[140] The aging physical plant, which had been poorly maintained for almost two decades, required a substantial investment, and the student-work program that had long been a hallmark of the institution was perceived as a financial drain. During the 1956 fiscal year, the schools' agricultural operations had a net loss of more than $26,000. The only aspect of the agricultural operations that posted a profit was the forestry unit, while the beef cattle, poultry, hog, dairy and other farm operations realized a net loss of over $100,000. The work program seemed to take precedence over the academic programs, but the work program was also diverting resources away from the primary business of the schools, which was education.[141]

The fall 1956 issue of the *Southern Highlander* featured an appeal to potential donors for contributions to help with operating expenses, such as salaries, equipment and building maintenance, as well as new buildings, including a dormitory, a warehouse, an administration building and staff housing. "The Berry Schools has been and still is an ideal campus," read the appeal, "offering its students all the advantages that a small high school and a small college give." Through its emphasis on religious life, Berry students had "been led to dedicate themselves to lives of Christian service," and through the work program, students had learned "the dignity of honest labor whether skilled or unskilled." But the school stood at a crossroads "in danger of progress passing it by" if it could not upgrade its facilities and increase the salaries of its underpaid staff.[142]

The issues and problems that occupied Berry's new president and its board of trustees throughout the mid-1950s and into the early 1960s, while critical for the future of the institution, were largely imperceptible to the boys on the mountain campus who continued to labor away at their work assignments and studies. Ron Pierce (60H) recalled that his mother read *Miracle in the Mountains: The Inspiring Story of Martha Berry's Crusade for the Mountain People of the South* when it was published in 1956 and promptly decided that the MBSB was a place that Ron "could have the right kinds of influences." "We were country folks," Pierce explained, and after his father died at an early age in 1952, his family found itself "suddenly living on Social Security." The MBSB offered "quite a bit of structure, a good clean environment, and a lot of exercise," remembered Pierce, adding, "I probably didn't have the best opportunity in the world to succeed in the environment I was in before I came to Berry." Despite the positive outcome for Pierce, who graduated from Berry College in 1974 and had a successful career as an educator, he acknowledged that the academic program at the MBSB always seemed to take a backseat to the work program. When alumni of the MBSB gather for reunions, said Pierce, "they all talk about their work, the growing up as a family, and living here in the dorms. They don't talk about academics."[143]

Although the academic program might not have been as strong as the school's leadership hoped, the MBSB was without question a refuge for many boys who attended the school. Reflecting on his time at the MBSB, Gene Price (56H) commented, "I wouldn't take a million dollars for the experience I had." The son of sharecroppers and the oldest of six children, Price arrived at Berry at the age of fourteen and began his time at the MBSB working full time at the dairy. Price was what was then known as a "regular worker," a student who worked full time for a semester in order to accumulate enough credit to take classes. The staff at the MBSB "basically raised us," said Price. "If we needed a father figure, there was one there. If we needed a mother figure, there was one of those. They were our surrogate parents."[144]

Students studying in Barstow Library, circa 1966.

The students relied on the faculty and staff for guidance, but the students were all a part of the support system as well. "If you needed a big brother or someone to talk to, there was always someone around," recalled Price. As an example, Price related the story of Charlie King (56H), who played the role of big brother at a time when Price himself became discouraged with life at the MBSB. During his first year at the MBSB, Price decided one evening that he would leave the MBSB the next morning, as soon as he finished his morning milking shift at the dairy. "I packed up my little ditty bag. My idea was when they came by at 3:30 to take me over to do the milking, I was going to go on over and do my little milking job, and when the truck came to bring everybody back to breakfast, I was going to head on out the stretch road and right on out the gate," said Price. As he exited his room in the wee hours of the morning, Price was stopped by King, who said, "Gene, you're not leaving until you have breakfast and you talk to me." Price marveled that King had seemingly read his mind, for he had told no one of his plan to leave the school. "It had to be divine intervention," said Price, "because I didn't tell him. To this day, I haven't figured out how he knew other than by divine intervention. I never said anything to anybody, and as far as I know, Charlie didn't either. I stayed and I graduated, and I'm proud of it."[145]

Not all the students behaved so nobly all the time, and some infractions could get a boy "shipped," as the students called expulsion. Grounds for expulsion included smoking, drinking or leaving the campus without authorization. Fighting, while frowned upon, would not necessarily get a student expelled. As Price noted, "You take as many kids as we had up here, somewhere along the way there's going to be a squabble." One memorable fight that did result in the shipping of Price's classmate Robert Weaver occurred when Weaver came out of the dining hall with a fork and started stabbing another boy. "That was the most serious thing I remember," said Price.[146]

One student was expelled after he broke into the dining hall after hours and drank a gallon of vanilla extract, recalled Don Collins (65A). Misbehaving in town was a shippable offense, said Collins, and over time, as the "squabbles" began to escalate, fighting became grounds for expulsion from the school.[147] Tom Butler (65A) cited stealing mail, drinking and riding the water wheel as transgressions that resulted in some of his classmates getting shipped.[148] John Shahan (64A) recalled a student getting expelled for shooting off firecrackers, adding that Fred Loveday had a way of getting the guilty party to confess. "He'd get us all up at 2:00 or 3:00 in the morning and bring us all in to the common room, and nobody went back to bed until somebody confessed. Who shot the fireworks? Who stole the tractor? Whatever was going on right then. He had a way of getting it out of you. Everybody was being punished as a group until somebody confessed," said Shahan.[149]

A frightening moment for Tom Butler and several other boys who were members of the varsity club occurred in the spring of 1965, just as the seniors were about to graduate. For many years, members of the varsity club had carried out initiation activities that involved having new members clean rooms, shine shoes, run errands, run laps around the athletic field and perform in front of the dining hall. The final indignity foisted on the initiates involved having them strip down to their athletic supporters; swallow raw eggs, raw oysters, vinegar and salt; and then lie down on the floor, face down, while a solution of carbon-disulphide was poured on each initiate's backside. The initiates were then required to jump in a barrel of water, which produced a chemical reaction with the carbon-disulphide and created "uncomfortable burning sensations lasting for a brief period of time provided the affected area was carefully washed immediately." Following the carbon-disulphide treatment, initiates were covered with syrup and told to roll in sawdust. They were then sent back to their dormitories to clean up. During the 1965 initiation, one of the initiates presumably failed to wash away the chemical mixture thoroughly, and he suffered second-degree chemical burns.[150]

After the injured student reported the problem to the school nurse, President Bertrand established a special committee to investigate the incident. "The bricks came down on us," recalled Butler, who was summoned to the recitation hall in the middle of the night to meet with members of the committee.[151] Most disturbing to the committee was the revelation that several faculty members had been involved in the incident. The coaches who were present when the hazing took place expressed apprehension about using the chemical, but they "went along" with the initiation because it was part of a varsity club tradition that had been in place for several years. The committee acknowledged that MBSB athletic teams "were well disciplined and represented themselves and the school well" but found it "inconceivable" that "faculty members of an institution would not only stand by and witness such a procedure, but also actually participate in it."

The final recommendations of the committee, which were approved by Bertrand, were the immediate elimination of the initiation procedures of the varsity clubs at both the high school and the college and the establishment of a public program for welcoming new members to the clubs. The committee stopped short of recommending that the faculty involved in the initiation be separated from the institution, feeling that the "best interests of the institution, the students, and the faculty members could be best served" by a severe reprimand rather than dismissal.[152] The students who were involved were not expelled, but they did collectively hold their breath for several days while the committee conducted its investigation and made its recommendations. "I thought it was all over," said Butler, "that I was about to get shipped off to military school somewhere."[153]

Whatever lapse in judgment the hazing incident represented for the coaches involved did little to diminish the high esteem in which the high school boys held the coaches. Jerry Shelton, a native of Fayetteville, Tennessee, had arrived at the MBSB to serve as an instructor of American government and physical education and to coach the baseball and basketball teams following his graduation from Berry College in 1958. He quickly gained the respect of his co-workers and, perhaps most importantly, of the boys because he was a disciplinarian. Shelton was demanding, recalled Don Collins, "but if you did what you were supposed to do, everything was OK. If not, there were consequences. He was tough but fair. He had things he wanted to accomplish, and we had respect for him."[154] "I learned a lot from Coach Shelton," said John Shahan, "basically how to win. He would never take less than 100 percent. He was a disciplinarian. He had us dress up in blazers—coats and ties. He instilled in us a confidence."[155]

"Coach Shelton taught me I could do anything I put my mind to," said Tom Butler, adding, "Athletics at Berry were transformative because it gave me a venue in which to succeed, and I had never had that before." In his senior year at the high school, Butler played on Shelton's basketball team that won a game in the regional playoffs against Cartersville High School in what was the longest game in Georgia high school basketball history at the time. "It was about midnight when we finished," remembered Butler of the game, which went into seven overtimes before the Berry boys emerged victorious. The victory at regionals led to a berth in the state tournament for the team known since 1960 as the Falcons. "Nobody on the team was really outstanding, but we had a great balance," Butler explained.[156]

Coach Shelton orchestrated many successful teams during his years at the high school. Reflecting on his time there, Shelton stated, "We had a special mission to fulfill. Many of the students were from broken homes and poor academic backgrounds. Many people had the perception that they were juvenile delinquents. My perception changed because I found that the students had overcome great obstacles in their lives. They had not had the opportunities that I had, but they were good people." The most rewarding aspect of working at Berry, according to Shelton, was "working with the students and reaping success." At the time of Shelton's arrival at the MBSB, Berry was still a closed society, much as it had been during Martha Berry's lifetime. Shelton was a pioneer in introducing the MBSB to the community and vice versa because of his role as athletic director. By engaging with other schools in the area through athletics, Shelton recalled, "the perception of the school changed. This was an opening of the school to the community. The students developed a great deal of pride in themselves and the institution." Shelton told them, "We're going to look better, act better and play better than anyone else," and the boys believed him.[157] Shelton left the high school to assume a coaching position at the college after the 1965 school year, but he left an indelible imprint on the lives of the boys whom he taught and coached between 1958 and 1965.

Opposite, top: Jerry Shelton receiving an award from Garland Dickey, circa 1968.

Opposite, bottom: The Berry Academy Falcons sign, a gift of the class of 1965, marked the entrance to the gymnasium and athletic fields for eighteen years.

The pride that Shelton instilled in his boys was perhaps never more evident than in the spring of 1965, when the graduating class gave as its senior gift a large metal sign designed by senior Vann Owens that read, "Berry Academy—Falcons," which was placed on the edge of the baseball field at the end of the "Stretch" road. The class had raised more than $250 to have the sign fabricated and had helped gather the fieldstones for the columns that supported the sign.[158] The sign would become a beloved symbol of the school.

Chapter 6

THE SHADOW OF THE PAST

Whereas the Berry College progresses because we know where it is going, the
Berry Academy lags behind because we know only where it came from.
—Laurence Campbell

The 1958 report of the Educational Advisory Committee offered broad recommendations for the Berry Schools in general but offered few specifics regarding improvements at the MBSB. Four years later, President Bertrand engaged the services of Dr. John A. Permenter, a well-respected public school administrator from Rockville, Maryland, to head a committee to carry out an in-depth look at the MBSB. The committee was made up of Permenter and five educators, most of whom were alumni of either the MBSB or Berry College. Bertrand asked the committee to "leave no stone unturned" in this study of the school. It was asked to inquire into the purpose of the MBSB, to study the curriculum, to evaluate the stability and qualifications of the staff and to ascertain what happened to the graduates of the school. According to Bertrand, the committee was to study "the total program of the school," including the work program, with the objective of making "recommendations for building an even more effective program (and giv[ing] more meaning to the Mount Berry School for Boys and its impact on the region)."[159]

Permenter and his team visited the MBSB in March 1963, and by May of that same year, the preliminary report on the school had been completed. The report identified the "ten areas of inquiry" on which the committee focused during its three days on campus as follows:

1. Purpose and mission of the Mount Berry School for Boys in the 1960s and beyond

2. Nature, scope, and quality of the instructional program

3. Adequacy of the staff; staff stability

4. Staff satisfactions and emoluments, living conditions, and morale

5. School spirit and morale

6. Nature and scope of the activities program, including recreational opportunities and social life

7. Religious, moral, and ethical values as propounded by the administration and as practiced by students and staff

8. The work experience program and its relevance to the school's present needs and to its philosophy and purposes; the educational and social significance of the work program to the individual student

9. School plant and teaching facilities

10. Administrative policies, procedures, and practices

The committee spent three days on the MBSB campus visiting classes, talking with students and staff and examining the facilities of the school. The committee reported that the administrators, teachers and students seemed unable to articulate "any clear-cut notion of a unique and unifying purpose being served by the Mount Berry School for Boys in 1963, particularly one based on the singular traditions and ideals that have been molded and manifested since the early days of the school." Identification of "a strong and unifying purpose that is in some positive way in keeping with its founder's vision and with the school's high ideals and noble traditions" was key to the ongoing success of the institution and "could restore some of the lost zeal and give definite direction to the school."[160] The MBSB's purpose, identified by most interviewees as "to be a good private college-preparatory school," was "too broad, too vague, and too commonplace," resulting in a school that offered nothing more than a program that was available in other private and public schools in the region. While such a purpose might have been "sufficient for most American secondary schools," wrote the committee, "it is not good enough for the school founded by Martha Berry."[161] The MBSB, it seems, had lost its way.

According to the Permenter report, the MBSB needed to establish a target demographic and focus on that demographic exclusively. Among the suggestions was that the school "might serve high-level-ability boys from broken homes" or that it could "become a school for problem boys." Either of these courses would require significant adjustments to the existing program. At the time, the school was perceived "as predominantly but not exclusively college preparatory." Approximately 60 percent of the MBSB's graduates were pursuing the college-preparatory course. The remaining 40 percent were taking the "general course," and according to the report, those boys were "ill-prepared either for future education or for suitable employment."[162] By trying to serve multiple purposes, the school was failing to excel at either. The general program seemed to be designed as a fallback for the students who could not succeed in the college-preparatory course, yet the general program offered the boys no vocational or technical training. According to the committee, "if the general course does not prepare a boy for college or for a vocational, technical, or semi-professional job, just for what does it prepare him?"[163]

Perhaps the most questionable program offering, according to the report, was the agriculture program. Deeply rooted in the school's history, the agriculture program was a four-year elective program for students pursuing the general course. The committee acknowledged that agriculture had once served as the principal program at the school but recommended that "despite its historical and emotional appeal," the program should be dropped immediately because there was "virtually no demand" for it. The industrial arts program, on the other hand, seemed to be of great interest to many of the boys pursuing the general course and was deemed to be providing limited "pre-vocational and technical training."[164]

Previous consultants had mentioned many of the same concerns that the Permenter committee raised in 1963, but none of the previous assessments had focused so specifically on the MBSB. Salaries for instructional staff seemed to be extremely low, and although most of the teachers were deemed to be "average or better," the committee observed that most of the teaching was highly conventional, and turnover among the faculty was "much higher than desirable."[165] Most of the staff felt that student discipline was not a serious problem and that the boys were "fairly easy to manage," although dormitory and other nonteaching duties, as well as unsatisfactory housing conditions for married teachers, were cited as burdens that contributed to the high turnover rate and the less-than-desired quality of classroom teaching.[166]

While morale among the faculty was reported as generally high, school spirit and morale among the students, according to staff and students interviewed by the committee, was the lowest ever. Students felt that what passed for student government was a "farce," serving merely as a "rubber stamp for an administration that has no intention or desire for the council to have any real power or influence." Many boys felt that the school was "too much out of touch with the outside world and with reality" and that upon graduation, they would not be well prepared to "face adult responsibilities."

Students leaving Friendship Hall, 1966.

Students in the common room of Pilgrim Hall in the 1960s.

The system of micromanaging the boys—telling them "what to do and when to do it"—robbed them of the opportunity to assume "progressive adolescent responsibilities."[167] The students felt that discipline at the school was handled in an unfair and inconsistent manner, and that transgressions should be punished as prescribed in the regulations.[168]

The boys also bemoaned the inadequate recreational facilities. The gymnasium was mentioned as the only facility for student recreation, but it was used primarily by the varsity sports programs. There were no tennis courts, swimming pool or satisfactory baseball and track facilities, according to the report. Even the facilities for less physically demanding recreation such as table tennis, billiards, checkers or chess were lacking. There were no televisions in the dormitories. There was, in short, very little recreational activity for the boys beyond the varsity and junior varsity sports teams.[169] The students were isolated on the mountain campus with very little connection to the outside world. And while one student reported that he came to the MBSB because of "the good boys here," others reported that "some boys learn to smoke and swear very quickly after coming to Berry." Smoking and swearing were considered by some of the students to be signs of low morals, and several students complained that "life at Berry does not have or develop the religious and moral character and strength" that they expected. If the boys were smoking and swearing, perhaps it was out of sheer boredom. "Many boys smoke here to be doing something besides studying, going to classes and working," commented a student, adding, "There is nothing much else to do here for fun or amusement."[170]

The work program was a topic that the committee described as "a perennial problem." Long the cornerstone of the Berry Schools, the work program "still weighs heavily in the whole Berry way of life," reported the committee, but it seemed likely that the program was "not nearly as economically defensible as the business manager would wish to see it, nor as educationally sound as the school principal would like."[171] As previous consultants had noted, the academic program was subordinate to the work program, and the educational value of the program was called into question. A closer alignment of work assignments with the educational program was recommended, with opportunities for outstanding students to serve as tutors, teaching assistants and laboratory aides.[172] The majority of the boys, however, were employed in the dining hall, the dairy or on the grounds crew—all pursuits that the consultants deemed questionable in terms of their educational and economical value for the students and the institution.

The harshest criticism was reserved for the administration, which the committee blamed for the laundry list of deficiencies and problems that it detailed in the report. From the lack of a unifying purpose to the weak instructional program and curriculum, the administration had much to answer for, wrote the committee, citing the instructional program as the "most serious administrative leadership failure." The committee reported that a "lack of vision and planning for necessary change," the failure to plan and budget for "essential improvements" and a "lack of determination and aggressiveness on the part of the school administration have all taken their cumulative toll."[173] There was "evidence that the principal does not communicate or try to communicate with the president well enough or often enough, nor with those in charge of business affairs and the work program" at the MBSB, and communication between the principal and the MBSB staff seemed problematic as well. The MBSB leadership was described as indecisive, inconsistent and unwilling to face reality and change. The committee concluded that the MBSB was "an average private college preparatory school unsure of what its guiding purpose and mission is or should be."[174]

Not one to hide from criticism, President Bertrand shared the report with Principal Fred Loveday, noting that the report was "critical of 'the administration,' a term which includes both of us." Bertrand seemed eager to discuss the report with Loveday, as well as with other members of the administration and the board of trustees.[175] In a note to Bertrand, new vice-president Tom Gandy indicated that he agreed with most of the committee's comments, especially regarding the purpose and mission of the school and the failings of the administration, adding that perhaps the major difficulty lay with the shortcomings of the administration, presumably referring to the principal.[176]

In an effort to respond to some of the criticisms leveled in the Permenter report of May 1963, the board of trustees began discussions about changing the name of the school from the Mount Berry School for Boys to Berry Academy. First raised at the June 8, 1963, board meeting, the name change was discussed and approved by the executive committee of the board in September 1963. According to Loveday, the MBSB name, which was unwieldy and had never been popular with the students, had a negative connotation in the community. Although the name Berry High School had been considered, Loveday felt that the name Berry Academy better showed the "difference between a private and public school." The executive committee agreed that such a name change was in order and voted to begin using the name in the 1964–65 catalogue.[177] The full board approved the name change in February 1964 and further voted to change the title of "principal" at the academy to "headmaster."[178]

Fred Loveday, who had served as the principal since 1947, was offered the new position of dean at the academy and was informed that he could apply for the headmaster's job if he so desired. Loveday did apply and was appointed headmaster in the spring of 1965. The administration also developed new parameters for student admissions, declaring in the late fall of 1963 that preferred admission at Berry Academy would be reserved for "especially able and purposeful boys irrespective of their financial means," with "preferred consideration given to prospective students" who met one of the following criteria:

1. from communities with inadequate public high schools

2. of parents whose religious, military or business duties require them to be out of the country

3. who might particularly benefit from a boarding-school environment, sons of ministers, missionaries, teachers, military men, and others whose work is of social consequence

4. whose education has been interrupted and who now, at an older age, wish to acquire as quickly as possible, the knowledge necessary to enter college[179]

At the same time that Bertrand was digesting the Permenter report in the spring of 1963, he was also wrestling with another problem related to the high school. Two boys who had repeatedly been caught off campus without permission were seen roaming the streets of downtown Rome on a Wednesday night. With their latest transgression, both boys exceeded the threshold for disciplinary action, which was one hundred demerits. Loveday had no choice but to suspend the boys, and he delegated to staff member Bill Green the responsibility for sending the boys home. On the morning of Thursday, May 30, Green drove the boys to the bus station and, according to Green, verified that they had enough money between them to purchase their bus tickets home. After securing a "solemn promise" from the boys that they would board the bus and go directly home, Green returned to the Berry campus, leaving the boys waiting for the bus.[180]

Much to the dismay of Green and Loveday, the boys did not board the bus as promised but instead hitchhiked to Atlanta. They were last seen about 11:00 p.m. near the corner of Tenth Street and Peachtree Road in Midtown. The parents of the boys had not been notified that the boys had been expelled but discovered this by accident when a girl who called looking for one of the boys mentioned that he had been "shipped." The father immediately called Loveday to inquire into his son's whereabouts. Loveday could only report that the boys had been dropped at the bus station at 9:35 a.m., but he agreed to notify the police about the missing boys. What happened next was the subject of some debate. Loveday claimed he contacted the county police and the Georgia Highway Patrol with a special request that the Atlanta Police Department be notified about the boys. The father of one of the boys claimed that Loveday had not notified the police. Although President Bertrand backed Loveday's claim, he was clearly distressed about the handling of the expulsion and the failure to ensure the return of the boys to their respective homes. The boys were finally located in Daytona Beach after Loveday intercepted a postcard from one of the boys to his former roommate. Bertrand later wrote to the mother of one of the boys and admitted that the school had handled her son's termination "in a very unsatisfactory manner and not in accordance with our standing policy." Bertrand indicated that the school would consider readmitting the boy on probation at the end of the summer if he proved "ready to apply himself at Berry and to observe our regulations."[181]

Bertrand's exasperation with what he perceived as a lack of discipline and control of the operations on the mountain campus had been increasing. The incident with the two boys who hitchhiked to Daytona Beach seemed to be the tip of the iceberg. In November 1963, Bertrand received a letter from the mother of an MBSB student who felt impelled to let the president know that the disciplinary situation at the high school was out of control. According to the mother, there was "no discipline in the dining hall except at noon time when Mr. Loveday is there." She wanted her son to learn good table manners and did not consider "laying [*sic*] on the table and fighting over the food [to be] basic good table manners." She also noted that the housemaster had been lax about room inspections and that the boys had reported on at least one occasion that the housemaster appeared to be drunk when he came through the hall for inspection. The mother had inquired about bringing these issues to the attention of someone in authority, but her son responded that such an effort was pointless because "no one cares." Noting that she "sent her son to Berry because it was considered the best place for him to learn to become a man and be able to take his place in this world," the mother reflected that "from the reports of the stealing, swearing and other things that go on, I now wonder." She concluded with a plea to Bertrand to show the boys that someone did care about them and their future.[182] In his response, Bertrand stated that, prior to receiving the letter, he understood the "problems of the kind you mentioned, which have plagued us in the past, had largely been corrected." He promised to investigate the situation personally and assured the mother that he and others at the school did "care very much" about the boys and the state of affairs at the high school.[183]

By December 1963, Bertrand felt that it was necessary to make an appearance at the mountain campus to address the disciplinary problems that seemed to be endemic at the high school. He appeared at noon in Hill Dining Hall on December 14, 1963, and announced that he was there to meet with the students and faculty to express his "concern about some matters of conduct." The list of transgressions was long and included fighting in the residence halls, hazing incidents, destruction of property in the dorms and classrooms, stealing, drinking and the use of foul language. Although Bertrand felt certain that "the vast majority of students, faculty and staff do not condone such actions," he thought it necessary to let everyone know that he did not approve of such behavior and that "effective immediately we will take all necessary steps to eliminate such actions at Berry Academy."

Addressing some of the specific steps that were to be taken, Bertrand stated that fighting, which had previously been tolerated to some degree, would now become grounds for immediate expulsion. However, students would be allowed to engage in "grudge" fighting under the supervision of a faculty or staff member as long as precautions were taken to guard against injuries. Bertrand added that immediate separation from the school was also the penalty for anyone who participated in or contributed to any of the aforementioned actions that were prohibited at the school, and he invited anyone who felt that they could not comply with this more strict enforcement of the rules to separate themselves voluntarily from the school during the Christmas holiday.[184]

In spite of the apparent increase in disciplinary problems that necessitated Bertrand's appearance at the high school in December 1963, there were some positive achievements in the 1963–64 school year. The high school was evaluated and reaccredited by the Southern Association of Colleges and Schools, and the name change from the Mount Berry School for Boys to Berry Academy seemed to be a resounding success. Special supervised study periods had been added in the evenings and resulted in an "improvement in academic achievement." One of the dormitories had been refurbished, and extensive improvements to the athletic facilities were underway. And as a particular point of pride, the athletic teams had won seven trophies, more than in any previous year in the school's history.[185]

The above successes, however, were not enough to convince Bertrand that the high school operation was on the right track. In 1965, he asked Dr. Laurence Campbell to make recommendations regarding the future of Berry Academy. Campbell, a well-known and highly respected educator who had spent a considerable amount of time at Berry in the late 1950s helping compile information for the school's accreditation report, submitted to Bertrand a ten-page memorandum that would provide much of the language that Bertrand would use when discussing the high school program in the coming years. Campbell was blunt and to the point, noting that the situation that had existed in 1902 when the school was founded no longer existed and that Berry Academy could not "be justified in terms of its role six decades ago." The board of trustees needed to choose between two options: either close the school or drastically redesign it through a complete overhaul of its entire program.[186]

Campbell stressed that "the non-public school must be different from the public school. And it must be better. Otherwise it really has no excuse for its existence...The 'plain truth,'" wrote Campbell, was "that Berry Academy has not been able to provide a better education than public schools. Whereas the Berry College progresses because we know where it is going, the Berry Academy lags behind because we know only where it came from. In one instance, we have looked ahead with courage; in the other we have looked to the past with caution." Campbell recommended that the school should continue to serve only male boarding students but that the focus shift completely to boys who wanted to prepare for college. He called into question the value of the work program, which had long taken precedence over the academic program, stating that the "work program today has little appeal" and that it is "by no means certain that boys who take part in the work program as now developed actually get enough out of it—except for the money they receive."[187]

Many alumni of the school at the time and today would consider Campbell's opinion to be heretical. The work program at Berry had been one of the cornerstones of the institution since its founding, and alumni today still reflect fondly on their work experience as one of the most meaningful parts of their time there. Nevertheless, the work program that had enabled the construction of the magnificent physical plant for which Berry was so renowned was repeatedly called into question as the school entered the second half of the twentieth century. Of greatest concern was that work schedules took precedence over class schedules. Each boy was expected to work eight hours a day two days a week and attend class four days a week.

However, oftentimes there was not enough work to occupy the younger boys for a full eight hours on their workdays. Instead of using that time for additional classes or studies, the boys were left to fend for themselves. This problem was addressed in more detail by another outside consultant, John C. Boggs, in a report delivered to Bertrand in the spring of 1966.

Boggs, the president emeritus of Randolph Macon Academy in Front Royal, Virginia, had visited the school in December 1965 at the invitation of Bertrand with the express intent of making "suggestions that could be considered by the Administration of Berry Academy in present and future planning." Boggs had more than forty-five years of experience in teaching and administration in private preparatory schools, and Bertrand believed that Boggs would bring an informed but objective eye to the knotty problem of what to do about the high school operation, which in Bertrand's view seemed to be floundering and had become a financial drain on the institution.[188]

Boggs generally commended the institution for its fine physical plant, noting that there were some facilities, such as laboratories and restroom facilities in the classroom building and locker rooms in the gymnasium, that needed updating. He noted the absence of furniture in the "common rooms" of the two dormitories, noting that these areas could serve as "attractive social centers and morale builders at comparatively little expense—equipped with book shelves, reading and game tables, television, etc." But the curriculum and the work program came under the most criticism. According to Boggs, "The Course of Study should be revamped and enlarged to meet the needs and requirements of the present educational age in which we live." Of greater concern was that the "actual schedule of the academic program, as well as other areas of school life, are directly affected by the Work Program." Students whose work did not fill the entire sixteen hours allotted to work each week left many of the younger boys as "free agents," noted Boggs, and enabled the boys to spend the time as they chose. "Such a situation furnishes grounds for developing habits far from conducive to good training and good results," explained Boggs.[189]

Another concern was that many of the boys who were "of low-grade academic interest and ability" felt that their "obligations as a student" extended only to their job performance and not into the classroom. There seemed to be little effort made to provide the necessary support to help these students succeed academically. Boggs suggested that the school develop a "regular academic and school week as practiced by other boarding, preparatory schools" and that the work program be designed to "fit into the academic and regular school program rather than a somewhat reverse approach existing at present."[190]

Addressing the subject of the student body, Boggs noted that much improvement was needed in both the quality of the students accepted at Berry and their behavior while enrolled there. He cited "the lack of proper haircuts and the wearing of tight and narrow trousers so prevalent in certain youth groups elsewhere, but having no place in a well-ordered school society" as a problem that affected the reputation of the school. The real problem, he said, lay in the too-low standards for acceptance at the school. "The administration has no real obligation to accept a student simply because application has been made," explained Boggs, and he recommended establishing a standing committee for review of applications, along with implementation of a testing program to determine scholastic aptitude and interest. The academy needed "a new approach to morale and pride in itself as a really good preparatory school," wrote Boggs, and "vigorous leadership in morale building and active planning to create and develop spirit appears to be seriously lacking." The school focused too much on its past, "where the mountain boy, with few outside contacts and advantages, was satisfied and happy in the environment of fifty years ago." But the boys now enrolled in the school did not come from the backwoods. Instead, they came from both rural and city environments that offered "modern advantages and disadvantages," and they were often not challenged with worthwhile activities during their off hours. Boggs reminded Bertrand that the old saying, "An idle brain is the devil's workshop," was trite but true and that the administration, faculty and staff needed to take a more aggressive leadership role in planning a complete program for the students at the academy. In closing, Boggs posited three possible courses of action for the school: maintain the present program, close the academy or continue under a revitalized approach such as that outlined in his report. Among his final recommendations was that the academy report to a separate board of trustees so that the school might move out from beneath the shadow of the college, which many years earlier had eclipsed the high school in terms of enrollment and reputation.[191]

Boggs's report was circulated to members of the board of trustees as well as to headmaster Fred Loveday and director of development John Lipscomb and vice-president Tom Gandy. Gandy responded to Bertrand in writing in December 1965, noting that Boggs had zeroed in on some of the core issues that plagued the high school operation. The work program, even though it was a fundamental part of Berry's educational

Fred Loveday and John Bertrand with honor graduates, circa 1961.

philosophy, needed to be modified. A student center and more structured activities, including intramural sports and possibly a football team, needed to be added. Tuition needed to be raised to cover the costs of educating the students. Most importantly, noted Gandy, something needed to be done about the headmaster. The current headmaster, Fred Loveday, "had too little experience except of one kind—all gained at Berry." Loveday needed "to be replaced with someone who has a far broader and more comprehensive outlook on the purposes of the academy," wrote Gandy. The school needed a headmaster who could "provide leadership for a much stronger academic program" and who had "enough stature to attract top-flight teachers." Gandy proposed that Loveday be moved to the alumni office as director of alumni affairs. The affection that many of the alumni felt for Loveday would make him a natural at cultivating relationships with former high school students, a segment of the alumni who had been neglected for many years.[192]

Director of development John Lipscomb agreed with much of Gandy's assessment, including his idea to move Loveday into the alumni office and conduct a search for a new headmaster. It was imperative, according to Lipscomb, that the change be made "in a way that would be fair to Fred Loveday and would not unduly alienate his host of friends among alumni and donors."[193] In a follow-up letter to Bertrand almost two months later, Lipscomb offered a job description for Loveday as assistant director of development that would have Loveday in charge of alumni affairs and responsible for fundraising for the academy. While Loveday's connections made him well suited for this job, according to Lipscomb, he expressed some concerns about Loveday's willingness to accept such a transfer. "After being captain of his own team for years," Lipscomb explained, Loveday "might not be especially happy in a subordinate position on another team."[194]

President Bertrand had for some time been considering whether to remove Loveday as headmaster. In November 1965, Bertrand and Gandy held a private conference with Loveday in which they confronted him about a variety of problems at the high school. Bertrand informed Loveday, "Several times during the past nine years, it has been necessary in my judgment to take action which you, as the person to whom I had delegated operational authority for the preparatory school program, should have taken. Several times I have requested you to keep me fully informed on all operational problems. Several times, in my judgment, it has been necessary for me to stipulate the enforcement of rules which we claimed were already those of the school." Borrowing from Laurence Campbell's report, Bertrand reminded Loveday that "the non-public school must be different from the public school. And it must be better," adding that the redesign and overhaul of the high school program that had been suggested six years earlier had proceeded much too slowly. Bertrand further reminded Loveday that it was unacceptable that he often learned about problems at the high school through the "grapevine" rather than directly from Loveday himself, citing the hazing incident that involved injuries to a student.[195]

In a report that he compiled in March 1966, Bertrand cited the Boggs report as evidence of the slow progress at the high school. Furthermore, the fiscal situation at the academy, which had been borderline for several years, had become dire in the 1965–66 school year. The academy had become a "deficit operation and a drain on The Berry Schools' operating funds and resources." Bertrand noted that there were scattered cases where the "headmaster did not provide sufficient information to parents or guardians of students having disciplinary problems" and that "surprisingly inadequate separation procedures were followed with students, and proper notification to parents and others was not made." Finally, there was evidence that the headmaster had made efforts to keep the president from learning about problems at the academy, at times even threatening to terminate anyone who informed the president of disciplinary problems or setbacks at the school.[196]

Some dates in the history of high schools at Berry

Martha Berry begins the Boys Industrial School on what is currently the south end of Berry's Lower/Main Campus.
The Martha Berry School for Girls opens on the Log Cabin Campus.
At Martha Berry's direction, Grady Hamrick starts The Mount Berry Farm School on the Mountain Campus for older boys.
The Mount Berry Farm School's name is changed to the Foundation School.
Clara Hall was completed as the first of the new Ford buildings for The Martha Berry School for Girls.
Freshmen and sophomore boys from the high school on the Lower Campus are moved to the Foundation School on the Mountain Campus as Berry Junior College is established.
The remaining boys from the high school on the Lower Campus are moved to the Foundation School on the Mountain Campus as Berry College is established.
The Foundation School is changed to The Mount Berry School for Boys.
The death of Martha Berry occurs.
The Martha Berry School for Girls closes.
The Mount Berry School for Boys is changed to Berry Academy.
Day students are first admitted to Berry Academy.
Girls are first admitted to Berry Academy.
The middle school at Berry Academy opens.
Berry Academy closes.

Alma Mater

Far up in the hills of Georgia stands
Old Berry, tried and true,
The Shrine of many a memory of
The Silver and the Blue.
Our loyalty and love we pledge,
God keep thee without fail.
Be thou the light that shines for right,
Alma Mater, Hail, All Hail!

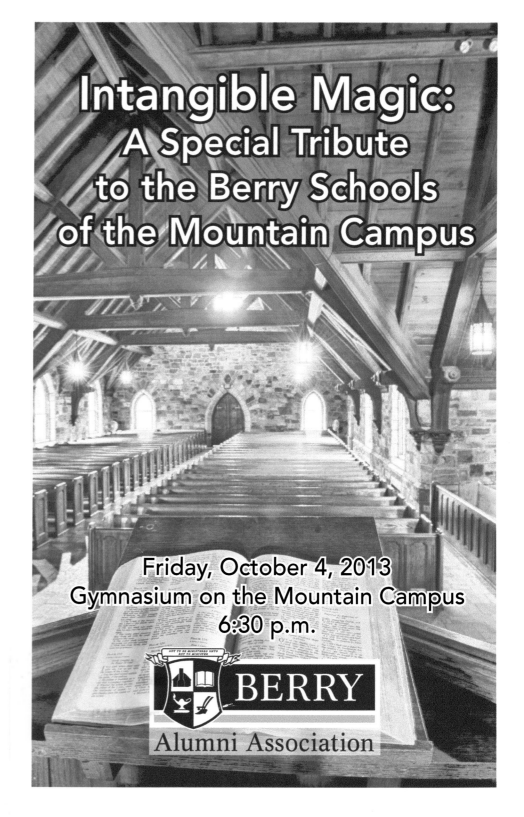

Intangible Magic:
A Special Tribute to the Berry Schools of the Mountain Campus

Friday, October 4, 2013
Gymnasium on the Mountain Campus
6:30 p.m.

BERRY
Alumni Association

Intangible Magic: A Special Tribute
to the Berry Schools of the Mountain Campus

Friday, October 4, 2013
Gymnasium on the Mountain Campus
6:30 p.m.

Presiding: Tom Butler (65A), President, Berry Breakfast Club

6:30 - 6:50 p.m.
Sign in.
Share and view items at the memorabilia table.
Mingle and reconnect with friends and classmates.

6:50 p.m.

Opening Remarks	Tom Butler
Welcome	Dr. Steve Briggs President, Berry College
Memorial Candle and Invocation	Larry Pierce (62H)

Dinner and Tribute to the Schools of the Mountain Campus

Introduction of author	Tom Butler
Words from the author of *A History of the Berry Schools* *on the Mountain Campus*	Dr. Jennifer Dickey (77A, 80C)
Introduction of speaker	Tom Butler
Guest speaker	Earl Tillman (52H) Past President, Berry Alumni Association

Remarks and Alma Mater	Haron Wis President, Berry Alum
Benediction	Rev. Billy E

Presentation of Gift from Berry
Berry will present as a gift to all attending alum
faculty and staff of The Mount Berry School for
Martha Berry School for Girls and Berry Acade
complimentary signed copy of *A History of the*
the Mountain Campus by Dr. Jennifer W. Dick

Book Signing by Dr. Jennifer W. Dickey

Additional copies of the book available for purch

View items at the memorabilia table.

Fireside Fellowship
Fellowship around the fire (designated area out
gymnasium) or inside. Musical instruments are

Miles

1902

1909

1916

1922

1925

1926

1930

1930

1942
1956
1964
1966
1971
1972
1983

Aln

On March 4, 1966, Bertrand met again with Loveday and informed him that, effective Monday, March 7, he would be transferred to the new position of assistant director of development. Loveday's salary would remain the same, and he would report to John Lipscomb. The new position, explained Bertrand, would be "a very vital one in the future of Berry Academy," and he felt certain that Loveday would "see the opportunity" available to him and the need that the school had for "a qualified person to fill the position." Unspoken in the meeting were the problems related to low enrollment (the high school enrollment in the 1964–65 school year had dropped to 144), the fact that key faculty members at the academy had threatened to leave if Loveday remained as headmaster and the need to mount a concerted effort to recruit faculty and students for the 1966–67 school year. Bertrand asked Loveday to refrain from discussing the matter with anyone outside his immediate family and offered Loveday time to think about his offer. Bertrand also informed Loveday that he did not have the option of continuing in his present position of headmaster at Berry Academy and that, effective March 10, Tom Gandy would take over as acting headmaster until the arrival of Robert Crawford from Maryland, who would serve out the remainder of the school year as interim headmaster.[197]

Loveday was no doubt shattered by his meeting with Bertrand. He had served at the high school in some capacity for twenty-four years, with the last nineteen years as either principal or headmaster. He was devoted to Berry, as was his wife, Mary, who taught Spanish at the academy. As many of the alumni would testify, Loveday was a beloved figure. However, much like Grady Hamrick before him, Loveday found that the school he had served devotedly for so many years was moving in a direction that the president and board felt Loveday was not prepared to lead.

Loveday initially responded to Bertrand that he would accept the transfer, but on Monday morning before Bertrand could announce the change, Loveday informed the faculty and staff at the academy that he was resigning as headmaster. Bertrand was incensed that Loveday had announced his resignation to the faculty and staff before informing him of his change of heart. Bertrand had prepared a statement to read at an assembly at the high school in which he pitched the reassignment in the most positive light, explaining that Loveday was the best person he could find to fill this new, important position that was so vital to the future development of the academy. Bertrand traveled to the mountain campus as scheduled around midday, but rather than announcing Loveday's transfer, he announced Loveday's resignation, adding that Mrs. Loveday had also resigned effective at the end of classes on that day.[198] Although Loveday's resignation was effective immediately, he and his family were allowed to remain in their on-campus home until mid-June so that his daughters could finish the school year. The Loveday family moved to the Atlanta area, where Mr. Loveday assumed the position of dean at the Lovett School and Mrs. Loveday taught Spanish.[199]

In a letter to his predecessor, Grady Hamrick, in May 1966, Loveday defended his time at the helm of the high school. He claimed the president gave no reasons for removing him as headmaster, adding that following a conversation with an unnamed source in the administration, he concluded that he was "forced out" because he "(1) had been late on some reports; (2) The president did not associate me with the Ivy League type of image he wanted the school to have; (3) That I was too devoted to the education of the underprivileged for him to build the kind of image he wanted for the school; (4) That the president expected to have another rise in tuition fee soon (presently $1,430) and that he was afraid that I would give him too much trouble on this score." Loveday further discussed how the administration, in his view, had failed to implement the president's 1959 recommendation that "no potential student who could benefit from the Berry Schools program and who has reasonable assurance of academic success should be denied the opportunity to attend because of lack of financial resources." The administration had not only failed to implement this recommendation, according to Loveday, but also had actually headed the academy "in the exact opposite direction." Loveday professed to be "completely confused as to what is the official direction of the school," adding that he felt that he "could operate as an educator on either plane—for the poor or for the not so poor. It would be impossible for Solomon to operate effectively in a muddled situation with the policy headed off in every direction. The charge to the alumni contained in Martha Berry's last letter—or my acceptance of this charge—has not been in my favor in the current relationships."[200]

Loveday's commitment to the spirit of Martha Berry's last letter, which had served him well for many years, proved to be his undoing in the final years of his time at Berry. As a graduate of the Berry Schools, Loveday was steeped in the history and tradition of the place. He believed in the work program and in the principle of providing an education to young boys regardless of their ability to pay, much as Martha Berry had done in the early years of the institution. The reports generated by the many consultants, from Victor Butterfield in 1942 to John Boggs in 1966, had all emphasized the need for the school to look to the future rather than the past to find its direction. While the college had begun to do just that, the high school had struggled to find its way.

Although Fred Loveday is remembered today by the boys under his charge as "a surrogate father figure" most of them sorely needed, the historical record indicates that many of the faculty and staff and some of the students had become disenchanted with Loveday's way of running things by 1966. Discipline, it seemed, had broken down considerably in the final few years of Loveday's tenure. A survey of the graduating seniors in 1966 indicated that there was great concern about the lack of discipline at the school and the uneven application of punishment for breaking the rules. Of greatest concern to the seniors was the "deficiency in the academic program and teaching"—problems that the consultants had raised repeatedly. Many students commented on the low morale at the school, and one student stated that "Berry Academy is hurting the name of The Berry Schools and should be closed down immediately."[201]

Fred Loveday was the last person to serve for more than six years as the leader of the high school. The school that was the direct descendant of Martha Berry's first boarding school would remain in existence for another seventeen years, and those years would be filled with more dramatic changes as the institution's leaders struggled to find a niche for the school on the mountain campus.

Chapter 7

A LEVEL PLAYING FIELD

I'll never give back to Berry what I took away from Berry. I'll never be able to repay what I got.
—Bob Williams, 62H

The 1960s were a tumultuous decade at the high school. The name change from the Mount Berry School for Boys to Berry Academy represented a philosophical shift, at least by the administration, in the school's mission. Although the leadership focused on making the change from serving as a school for poor boys who had limited educational opportunities to that of a college preparatory academy, the shift in the academic program seemed almost imperceptible to most of the boys enrolled in the school during the transition. Reflecting on their time there many decades later, almost all of the alumni recall fondly their participation in the work program and the sense of community that they felt at Berry. Few of them remember the low morale or lack of discipline that seemed to permeate the school during this period of time; instead, they recall how their experiences there prepared them for their lives.

In many ways, the boys who attended the high school in the 1960s during the transition from the MBSB to Berry Academy represent the last generation of students who fit the profile for which the school was first created more than half a century earlier. They were the last of the students who, as a whole, came from disadvantaged or difficult circumstances and for whom the work program made their education possible. Former student John Shahan (64A) remembered being "one of the last poor boys who worked their way through school. We didn't have any money, and we couldn't afford anything. We were just glad to be at Berry." According to Shahan, many of the disciplinary problems that arose in the 1960s were related to the changeover from the MBSB to Berry Academy. After the school became Berry Academy, said Shahan, more students who could afford to pay for school began to arrive, and apparently "those boys had money, and I guess they knew how to buy beer."[202]

Bob Williams (62H) was in many ways representative of the boys who attended the MBSB prior to the shift to a college preparatory program. The son of a sharecropper, Williams arrived on the mountain campus in the fall of 1958. The MBSB gave Williams a much greater sense of community than did life on the farm where he grew up. "There was not a lot of socializing outside the farm," said Williams, adding that at Berry, "I didn't feel isolated. I had more friends at Berry than on the farm." Like many of the boys, he worked full time his first semester at the school. Williams's first job was in the dining hall under the tutelage of Clifford "Judge" Hill, whom Williams described as "rugged" but "fair." "You knew what your job was" with Hill, recalled Williams. After working for two years as a pastry chef in the dining hall, Williams was transferred to the poultry farm under Kenneth Wehunt. After two weeks of training at the poultry farm, Wehunt handed Williams the keys and left him in charge. The trust shown by Wehunt proved to be a great motivator for Williams and his co-workers. "We worked harder than if he had been there," said Williams.[203]

Hill and Wehunt were not the only influential adults for Williams. Biology teacher and coach Raymond Douglas and coach Jerry Shelton were role models. "What I learned and gained through athletics was most meaningful," Williams stated. "I didn't have a lot of natural ability, so I had to work hard. Coach Shelton taught me a lot about perseverance. If I had to give credit for learning to one person, it would be Jerry Shelton." Williams felt that "the teachers were good, and they did it because they loved it, not for the pay. The teachers raised us," he said, "and if we had problems, we went to them." Recalling his struggles with his English teacher at the MBSB, Williams commented, "I could have killed him in high school, but I wanted to hug his neck when I got to college."[204]

Like most of the boys at the MBSB, Williams had little money and would have had limited opportunities to pursue an education and participate in such extracurricular activities as basketball and baseball had it not been for Berry. The MBSB not only gave him an education but also instilled in him through both the work program and athletics a work ethic that contributed to much of his later success. It also gave him a "family" to whom he still feels connected. His time at the MBSB was transformative, and reflecting on it, he commented, "I'll never give back to Berry what I took away from Berry. I'll never be able to repay what I got."[205]

Among the students who arrived at the MBSB as the transition from the MBSB to Berry Academy began was Tom Butler (65A). Looking back on his time there, Butler recalled that "the name change to the academy gave a different perception to people in the community," even if the shift to a college preparatory program was not wholly evident to the students. Butler arrived at the MBSB in 1961 after his father committed suicide and his mother moved to New Orleans to go back to school. "My family fell apart," said Butler, "and my mother was looking for a place to put me. I was thirteen years old and didn't want to come, but I got here and realized that just about everyone here had some kind of crazy story. Just nobody talked about it much. Many were much worse than mine. One guy had been tortured. One of my really good friends had just been dropped at the gate." In spite of his reticence about coming to the MBSB, Butler soon found his place, and his experience changed his life. "The men there during those four years taught me how to be a man of character," recalled Butler. "Different people taught me different things," Butler explained, citing Fred Loveday as the person who taught him to respect authority, his work supervisors with teaching him how to work and Jerry Shelton as the person who taught him how to be successful and to persevere.[206]

Although he admitted that the academic program was weak, noting that he felt unprepared for college when he arrived at Mercer following his graduation from Berry Academy, Butler remembered his teachers as "heroes" who, in spite of the fact that they did not make much money, took a real interest in the students. "I would have been a lost child," said Butler, adding, "The things you acquire when you're thirteen to fourteen years old lay the foundation." Reflecting on what his time at Berry meant to him, Butler stated, "I've always thought of it as a sacred and holy time for me. I can just drive through the gate, and I feel that spiritual connection to my past, and I go back. What was happening out on that mountain saved lives and sent people out into the world who have made a difference in the world."[207]

One of Butler's classmates, Don Collins (65A), arrived at the MBSB in January 1962. For Collins, the transition to the MBSB was difficult. Arriving in mid-year following his parents' divorce, fourteen-year-old Collins recalled that he did not feel as if he fit in for the first several months. He had two roommates who had been together since the beginning of the school year.

But by the end of his freshman year, recalled Collins, he had begun "counting the days until I could come back." Like many of the alumni from this period, Collins remembered more about his work assignments than he did about the academic program. One of his assignments was at the chicken farm, where he had to collect the eggs each morning. Along with collecting the eggs, he had to "dispose of any chickens that had expired overnight," recalled Collins, "and then you'd go to lunch and find out you were having fried chicken. The last thing you wanted to see was a fried chicken!" Recalling Mr. Loveday, Collins said, "He let me know that I was there at the school's pleasure, not my pleasure." The fear of being "shipped" kept Collins largely on the straight and narrow path, and the work program imparted to him the same life lessons it imparted to Tom Butler and many of his classmates. "God puts you where you need to be," said Collins, adding, "I come back about three times a year just to renew my soul."[208]

Arriving as a freshman at the MBSB in 1963, Luis Leon was one of the first Hispanic students at the high school. A native of Cuba, Luis Leon was one of more than fourteen thousand children transported to the United States between 1960 and 1962 as part of Operation Peter Pan. The unaccompanied minors were sent to the United States by their parents in an effort to have them escape the Communist revolution in Cuba. Most of the children were resettled with foster families until their parents could join them, something that did not begin to happen until the Freedom Flights in 1965. Leon, who was twelve when he arrived in the United States in 1961, moved in with a foster family in Miami, where he stayed for two years. When he turned fourteen, Leon left his foster family to attend the MBSB. Describing the situation he encountered upon his arrival at the MBSB in 1963, Leon explained, "It was a level playing field. No one had their parents. We were all in the same boat." For Leon, Berry was a great equalizer. He was one of eight or nine Cuban refugees enrolled at Berry. "We were the brown kids," he recalled, "part of an effort to diversify the student body, part of the integration process."[209]

For Leon, being away from his parents at the MBSB was not traumatic—he had left them behind two years before he arrived at Berry. "I never felt that the other students looked at us as outsiders," recalled Leon, adding, "Most of them were very friendly." Like his classmates, Leon recalled fondly the sense of community at Berry. He also remembered his time there as one of transition, during which the school made an effort to improve the quality of its teachers. "The new teachers were definitely a step up," according to Leon, who felt generally well prepared for college by the time he graduated,

Map of the Berry Schools showing Berry Academy on the mountain campus, 1966.

although he lamented that he was not exposed to Shakespeare in any of his high school English classes. "I really scrambled in English when I got to Sewanee and had to read Shakespeare," said Leon, noting, "I felt really well prepared in math and science and history, but not English." Leon remembered science teacher and track and cross-country coach Gary McKnight most fondly, stating that "we would have run through a wall for him, but he would never have asked us to." He added, "He had the greatest impact on my life."[210]

Like the other boys during this period, Leon participated in the work program—something that he credits with teaching him some of the most important life lessons that have led to his success. Recalling his varied assignments on the grounds crew, the chicken farm, the dining hall and in the office, Leon explained that the work program "gave me a work ethic and discipline and taught me to show up on time. It taught me that you don't start at the top; you work your way up. If I had wished anything for my daughters," Leon said, "it would be for that experience."[211]

By the time Luis Leon graduated in 1967, Berry Academy had not only repositioned itself as a college preparatory school, but it had also begun accepting day students, something that would change the atmosphere on the campus. Not only were the day students generally more affluent, but they could also come and go from the mountain campus as they pleased— something that the boarding students could not do. The sense of isolation and community that had been part of the core experience for so many of the boys in years past would begin to fade away as the school moved into the new era with a new name, a new headmaster, a revised curriculum and a changing student body. The high school would operate for twenty years as Berry Academy, but never again would it have the same transformative effect on young lives that it did during the first six decades of its existence.

Chapter 8

TRADITIONS AND TRANSITIONS

We don't ever want to abandon anything Miss Berry started.
She was always ahead of her time.
—*Frank Campbell*

The transition at the academy following Fred Loveday's departure was carried out as planned with educator Robert Crawford filling the role of interim headmaster from March 15, 1966, until June 30, 1966. Following his short stint at the helm of the school, Crawford drafted a report intended to help guide the leaders at Berry as they attempted to move forward with developing the high school into a reputable college preparatory institution. Addressing the work program, Crawford acknowledged that "its usefulness in today's society has been questioned" and that there was a groundswell of support for dropping the work program. The lack of flexibility within the work program had "reduced the quality of academic work while at the same time creating a disciplinary problem," according to Crawford. The program was part of the rich tradition of the institution, noted Crawford, and there were "many 'old Berry boys' who still regard it as the medium through which they threw off the shackles of ignorance and became understanding and contributing citizens of modern society." They loved the work program, and they looked to it "to do for their sons what it did for them." The academy could "ill-afford to take action that would antagonize or alienate this staunch group of alumni," wrote Crawford, suggesting that some middle ground might be tried that continued the work program but on a basis that was secondary to the academic program. Students should attend classes five days a week, with work scheduled a maximum of two hours a day during the week and on the weekends. The academic program should be streamlined and strengthened, and the rules and regulations of the school needed to be fairly and uniformly enforced.[212]

Crawford's recommendations aligned almost perfectly with those of Boggs, and the administration seemed committed to carrying out many of the recommendations. The job of implementing this plan fell to Frank Campbell, who assumed the role of headmaster at Berry Academy in July 1966. Campbell had served as a teacher and principal in the public school system for fifteen years before coming to Berry College as director of admissions in 1962. Campbell realized that the academy was a troubled operation, but he accepted the challenge to try to develop a college preparatory program at the school. Four months into the job, Campbell shared with President Bertrand his observations about the academy in an effort to establish a baseline from which he felt he could measure the success of the school going forward. According to Campbell, "The academy would not compare favorably with the better public high schools in the area in fulfilling its role as a college preparatory school." Although the academic program had been changed to five days a week, it still needed significant improvement. Only a few seniors from the academy could even be considered for admission to Berry College, according to Campbell, and students from the area public schools had superior records to those of the students who had graduated from the academy over the past four years.[213]

Campbell reported that not only were the students not up to par academically, but they were also poorly motivated and undisciplined. Berry Academy needed "many more serious-minded and capable students in order to establish a reputation as a first-rate college preparatory school," according to Campbell. The school needed to adopt a much more selective admissions process, and the administration needed to be prepared for the high school to operate at an enrollment level considerably below capacity for a period of three to four years while the quality of the students was upgraded. Only about 80 percent of the students were now participating in the work program, which had been made optional and modified to accommodate the new five-day-a-week class schedule. Although Campbell considered the faculty to be one of the "outstanding features" of the school, he felt it imperative that more on-campus housing be made available for the faculty so that they could be more engaged with the school and the students, especially with extracurricular and evening activities. The isolation of the

Graduation at Frost Chapel in the 1960s.

school at the base of Lavender Mountain, which had been such a selling point in the past, had become a liability for recruiting new faculty as limited on-campus housing options forced many teachers to face a long commute from off campus each day.[214]

Another significant change for the 1966–67 school year was the admission of day students to the academy. While the children of Berry faculty and staff had always had the option of attending the MBSB or the academy as day students, the school had never before accepted day students from the Rome community. Sixteen boys enrolled at the academy as day students in the first year the school began accepting them as such. Tuition and fees, including noon meals, books and transportation for day students, were $894. Boarding

119

Mary Todd Harrison assists students in English class, 1967.

students paid $1,430 for an academic year, an amount that Campbell considered much too low if Berry Academy wanted to position itself as a good-quality college preparatory school. A survey of fifteen boys' secondary schools in the Southeast indicated that the median tuition for an academic year at comparable private institutions was $2,200.[215]

In a memo to Bertrand in December 1966, Campbell recommended that the academy raise its tuition to $2,000 for boarding students and $1,000 for day students. "Berry Academy cannot continue to exist as an institution providing 'free' or low-cost education to boys who would not otherwise receive an education," wrote Campbell, adding that "reasonably good public schools are now available to every boy in every community. A private school must fill a need that public schools cannot meet; it can no longer substitute for non-existent public education." The school had to choose between serving boys who were "not acceptable in public schools or their own homes" and "students whose parents desire them to have the advantages that good private schools are equipped to provide." The latter category was, in Campbell's opinion, the "type of education for which Berry has always stood," and it was incumbent on the leadership to make sure that the school continued to fulfill this mission. The current low tuition was actually a "deterrent to the enrollment of good students," according to Campbell, because parents and students were "suspicious of 'bargains' in a matter as important as education."[216]

In his annual report to the president in August 1967, Campbell noted that the previous year had been a "crucial one in the history of the institution" and that many more changes would be required "if the academy is to survive and retain its position as an institution contributing to education and a better society." Among his observations after his first full year at the helm of the school was that the increase of tuition for the academic year to $2,000 for boarding students had served to improve the quality of applications for the upcoming year. The increase helped "eliminate applications from 'bargain hunters' who are not really interested in excellence in education, and improve the school's image." In spite of this improvement, "the image of Berry Academy in the minds of the public and prospective students has presented a serious problem," reported Campbell, and "many more applications must be received before the academy can select a sufficient number of well-motivated boys with adequate ability for a good academic program." Indeed, enrollment had dropped from 144 the previous year to 137 in the 1966–67 school year. However, a greater percentage of the academy's graduates (82.9 percent versus 75.5 percent) were entering college. Continued improvement of the academic program, along with a more selective admissions process, would be the key to success, according to Campbell.[217] The academy offered a "worthwhile program in a splendid setting," wrote Campbell, who claimed to be more optimistic after his first full year as headmaster than he had been after the first six months, and he needed the administration only to remain patient as he implemented the proposed changes.[218]

Campbell remained at Berry Academy until 1971. During his tenure, the school made great progress toward improving its reputation as a true college preparatory school. While he spent a great deal of time dealing with such large issues as revamping the academic program and developing tougher admissions standards, he also had to deal with the minutia of running a boarding school that was operated at a remote location in aging buildings. A letter from senior Tom Dabney in January 1968 offers a glimpse into some of the day-to-day problems confronting Campbell. In a polite but desperate plea to Campbell, Dabney requested that the senior boys who lived in Friendship Hall be given soap dishes for the showers, lighting in the common room (apparently only four of sixteen bulbs in the common room chandelier actually burned) and bulletin boards in the area around the phones. Dabney was also concerned about the poor job being done by the housekeeping crew in Friendship Hall.[219]

Students walking from the classroom building to the dining hall, circa 1969.

Campbell responded the same day to Dabney's letter, promising to remedy these problems.[220] That such basic maintenance issues were being overlooked and that a student felt compelled to write such a letter to the headmaster is telling of both the lack of attention to detail and the sense that students felt Campbell to be, at least, approachable and willing to deal with such problems. Around the same time, another student wrote to Campbell that at the academy "there is no spirit, no binding force to hold the students together." The place was "dead," according to the student, and "nothing of interest happens often enough to make students enjoy going to classes."[221] Boosting morale was an ongoing battle for Campbell, and the issues that affected the mood of the students varied from church attendance to feelings of indignity by the students related to regulations of their personal appearance.

For the first time in many years, a Student Government Association became active at the academy. Its president, Jack Pigott, held the administration's feet to the fire on a number of issues. Pigott informed Campbell that the lack of faculty attendance at the weekly on-campus church services was undermining one of the basic tenets of the school's mission, that of religion in life, and that it was the responsibility of the faculty and the students to support this important aspect of campus life.[222] Pigott also requested that the dormitories be inspected for fire safety and that the students have access to fire extinguishers. "We feel that this equipment should be standard and that it should not be forced upon the students to ask or even beg for instruments which may save their lives," wrote Pigott.[223]

Other shortcomings at the academy included inadequate common rooms in the dormitories, the lack of a recreation center and the need for an upgraded curriculum. "How can a top notch school obtain top notch students without top notch courses and teachers," wrote Pigott in a letter to President Bertrand in May 1968, adding, "More quality students need to be obtained" and the school needed to "work toward building a better faculty."[224] Student James Leppard III complained to Campbell that recent attempts to regulate haircuts at the school was "an irrationally directed attempt at authority at the wrong time" and that such regulation was a violation of the rules as stated in the Berry Academy Student Handbook.[225]

A little more than a year later, Bertrand established a Berry Academy Student Advisory Committee to the President in an effort to improve communication between the academy students and the administration. A team of thirteen students composed of the student government officers, the presidents of the four classes, the editors of the student publications and one representative from each of the dormitories and the day students was to meet with the president biweekly to have "an in-depth discussion of current concerns to Berry Academy students." Bertrand reminded the students that they were expected to abide by the rules that were currently in place but that the new advisory committee would be the venue for presenting concerns and recommendations regarding rule changes at the school. The students were promised a new activity center on the first floor of Cherokee Lodge, as well as more social activities on the campus, with the hope that "perhaps someone could interest some real, live girls in coming to more dances at Berry Academy!"[226]

While wrestling with these student concerns, Campbell and Bertrand were also dealing with some major problems, such as the academy's budget deficit and how to increase enrollment while upholding the school's admission standards. The college was operating at a deficit as well, but the per-student deficit for the college was $375 as compared to the academy's deficit of $1,100 per student for the 1967–68 school year.[227] As had been the case for many years, funds from the school's endowment were being used to supplement the cost of operating the school. Because low enrollment continued to plague the institution, Campbell and the administration entertained a variety of options to get more students in the door without lowering the admission standards. A plan to recruit high-achieving day students from the overcrowded public school system was begun, as were discussions about admitting female day students.

Enrollment for the 1968–69 school year was 112 students. A dramatic increase (48 percent) at the beginning of the 1969–70 school year, however, seemed a harbinger that the school was about to turn the corner. After four years of enrollment declines attributed to "the shifting of emphasis to a college preparatory program and a more careful selection of students to fit this new program," it appeared that the planned transition was on track. The number of day students had increased to 35, and according to Bertrand, "the academy appears to be projecting a favorable image locally." As the school prepared for reevaluation by the Southern Association of Colleges and Schools in 1970–71, Bertrand declared, "We have resolved the question of what kind of school the academy is to be. We now need to determine what size school it is to be—with present facilities, or with modifications or additions of existing facilities—to operate most efficiently."[228]

Further discussions on this subject would result in a recommendation from Campbell and John Lipscomb to Bertrand that the optimum enrollment for the academy was 180 students with no more than 50 day students, given the school's current facilities. Campbell and Lipscomb also suggested that although serious consideration should be given to admitting female day students, such a step should not be taken until the maximum enrollment of boys had been reached.[229] "It would be easy to fill the school with twice as many students as we have now if we just weren't so particular and selective," explained Campbell a year later, noting that about 96 percent of the class of 1970 had been accepted to college. "Five years ago, I don't think you would have found many Rome families interested in sending their sons to this school," adding that one-third of the student body was now day students. Responding to a question about changes to Berry's basic philosophy, Campbell commented, "We don't ever want to abandon anything Miss Berry started. She was always ahead of her time. We are the ones who got behind the rest of the world when Miss Berry died in 1942. She was such a forceful person that her death left everyone floundering for a while."[230]

Another consideration was how to deal with the matter of integration at the academy. Berry College had admitted three African American students in the fall of 1964 without incident, but the academy had remained an all-white institution until 1968, when Roy Lee Hunter attended for a year before enrolling in Berry College. No sustained effort had been made to recruit black students at Berry Academy, and as John Lipscomb noted in a letter to President Bertrand in February 1970, it seemed unlikely that the school would "be able to enroll any significant number of qualified Negro students at Berry Academy unless we make a special effort to attract them." It would likely be necessary "to offer generous scholarships to some good prospects until we have established an integrated image," offered Lipscomb, noting that it was important for academy students to have the experience "of attending an integrated school," that Berry needed to "avoid the possible appearance of being an anti-integration independent school" and that if the school did not take the initiative on its own, it would soon be forced "to show good faith efforts to integrate."[231]

Lipscomb's concerns about Berry Academy's being perceived as an "anti-integration school" were not without merit. In the wake of the 1954 *Brown v. Board of Education* decision by the U.S. Supreme Court, which ruled that separate public schools for black and white children were unconstitutional, "private academies" had become the refuge for white families in places like Prince Edward County, Virginia, who did not want to send their children to integrated public schools. Berry, of course, had long been a private school, and although its official admission publications made no reference to race or creed, the public perception was that Berry was a school for whites. "I always thought private schools were for rich kids to get away from integration," said Reggie Owens, who was admitted to the academy in the fall of 1971. Owens, a freshman from Cedartown, Georgia, was one of four African American students who enrolled in the academy for the 1971–72 school year. Dennis Shropshire, Gary Hill and Troy McCrory, all of whom had previously attended public schools, transferred to Berry Academy because they felt that they could get a better education there than they could at the public schools they had previously attended.[232]

The four students approached the beginning of the school year with some degree of trepidation. "I was expecting to find rich snobs," said Hill. "But when I talked with some students, they were really pretty good fellows and very friendly. I wanted to come because I thought a preparatory school education would give me a better chance to enter college. But I didn't really expect to be accepted by Berry. I was really surprised." McCrory had applied to Berry Academy to avoid having to go to school at East Rome High, where his mother was a teacher. "I didn't like going to school where she taught," he said, adding, "I think I'm getting a better education here, too." Owens had been worried that "some big, bad racist might put me in the hospital," but his fears disappeared after he arrived at the academy. "The only problem I had," he commented, "was before I realized that seniors have top priority."[233] Much as the college had done, the academy crossed the integration hurdle with little fanfare.

As the school eased into the 1970s, the issue of haircuts, which had been raised previously as a student concern, became a matter of increasing attention. During the 1971 calendar year, half a dozen memos flew back and forth between the academy and the president's office about the school's policy on haircuts. New dean of students Richard Ingram reported to Bertrand in January 1971 that the past and current policy was "off the collar, off the ears, and out of the eyes." Students were apparently taking issue with this policy, but Ingram recommended that it remain in place.[234] Headmaster Campbell endorsed Ingram's recommendation, noting, "I do not believe we can continue to recruit the type of student that we would like to have at Berry Academy unless their parents see a neat and well-groomed student body." The academy had about twenty students whom Campbell considered to be in violation of the haircut regulations, and "immediate enforcement of the regulation" was necessary unless there was an agreement reached on a new policy.[235] Discussions about how to deal with haircuts continued throughout the year and into the summer.

When Frank Campbell, who had served as headmaster at the academy for five years, departed to pursue a doctoral degree in the summer of 1971, he was replaced by Dr. John Permenter, the MBSB and Berry College alumnus who had been a member of the study team that Bertrand had invited to review the school in 1958. Permenter had recently retired from his position as deputy superintendent of schools in Montgomery County, Maryland, and agreed to return to Berry as the new academy headmaster. At Permenter's suggestion in September 1971, Bertrand authorized a new policy, to be enforced by a three-person committee consisting of the dean of the academy and two students, which focused not on the length of the students' hair but on "cleanliness, neatness, and attractive grooming of the hair."[236] The relaxing of the rules regarding hair length proved to be short lived, however, and by December, Ingram issued a memo to the students notifying them that "young men at the academy will have their hair styled in such a way as not to extend in length below the collar of a dress shirt." The boys were still expected to keep their hair "clean and well-groomed at all times." And although the students were no longer required to wear uniforms as they had done in the past, they were expected to adhere to the dress code spelled out in the student handbook. Ingram also expressed "deep concern about possible drug and alcohol abuse at the academy" and requested the cooperation of all students and staff in dealing with such problems.[237]

Prior to his departure from the academy, Campbell had engaged with Bertrand in discussions about some of the significant problems that plagued the Berry Schools, such as ongoing budget deficits, long-range planning of Berry's "total program" and the "lack of sufficient enrollment at both institutions to utilize fully the existing facilities." One suggestion that had arisen was to relocate the academy to the Ford campus and use the mountain campus for other purposes. In a memo to Bertrand in January 1971, Campbell posited that, while moving the academy operation to the Ford campus would not be difficult "from a facilities standpoint," some detailed studies would be needed to ensure that the Ford complex could accommodate the needs of the high school. Campbell assumed that Clara Hall could accommodate all of the boys who were presently residing in the Pilgrim and Friendship Hall dormitories on the mountain campus, but he had concerns about the commingling of high school boys and college girls that would take place at the Ford complex with college girls continuing to reside in Mary Hall to use the Ford gymnasium facilities.[238]

Campbell acknowledged that "consolidation of facilities should result in substantial monetary savings to both the college and academy," that the facilities at the Ford complex were "generally superior to those at the academy and could be developed into a superior secondary school" and that the "more accessible location should make it easier to attract larger numbers of local students—especially girls, if the academy became coeducational." There were, however, some disadvantages associated with consolidation, such as the aforementioned issue of high school students mixing with college students and possible scheduling conflicts with some of the facilities. Furthermore, the isolation of the academy was advantageous from an educational standpoint, according to Campbell, and moving the high school to the Ford campus "would make the academy more like urban-area independent schools with some of the accompanying pressures and problems. The pace of life would be accelerated." Campbell's last point was that closing the academy campus and "consolidation of the college and academy on the college campus could present a public relations problem with alumni, the general public and students." Were it necessary to consolidate the schools, however, Campbell suggested that consideration be given to establishing a country day school on the mountain campus. Recalling Martha Berry's original "Foundation School," which she had established at the mountain campus some fifty years earlier, Campbell argued that such a school could be a "feeder elementary school" to a coeducational academy and college.[239]

Discussions about relocating the academy continued into the spring meeting of the executive committee of the board of trustees, but the committee decided not to proceed with the consolidation. Within a few years, much of the "excess capacity" that had been such a great concern at the college had been filled by enrollment increases to the point where the college had to set up modular units just west of Hermann Hall to accommodate its female boarding students.[240] The academy students remained sequestered on the mountain campus, but major changes were about to happen.

Although enrollment had increased considerably under the leadership of Frank Campbell, the school had still failed to reach the optimum enrollment of 180 students. In the spring of 1971, 164 boys were enrolled in the academy. Almost 30 percent of the students were local day students, a segment that Campbell felt could be expanded significantly if girls were to be admitted to the school. Campbell's recommendation to accept "qualified girls" from the local community for all grade levels was approved in the spring of 1971, and in August 1971, the *Rome News-Tribune* announced, "Berry Academy to admit girls for first time." According to Headmaster Permenter, the caliber of the young ladies who applied to the academy was very impressive, and he expected coeducation to "add considerably to the quality of both our academic and social life."[241] Fifteen girls enrolled in the academy in the fall, making the boy-to-girl ratio at the school nine to one. While the girls seemed to blend in nicely and enjoyed the favorable odds, the consensus among the boys was, "It's great having girls around, but there really aren't enough yet to go around." Student Dick Muller seemed to think that having girls on campus improved morale and helped the school spirit. Dennis Shropshire commented, "This year we have our own cheerleaders, and it will mean a lot to the team." Debbie Morris, one of the new coeds, noted that there was a strong atmosphere of "togetherness" at the academy and that it seemed more like a big family than a school. Libbie Case agreed, commenting that "Berry seemed to be a bunch of kids getting together to learn but also to have fun at the same time." Jenny Brock observed that "the students and teachers are sincere in their willingness to help the girls feel comfortable in their new school."[242]

In spite of the addition of girls to the campus in the fall of 1971, enrollment was down slightly to 149 students at the beginning of the year. By November, 10 students had been dropped from the rolls for myriad reasons, including drugs, theft and, in one case, death. By the end of the calendar year, John Permenter had decided that serving as headmaster of the academy was not something he wanted to do, so dean of students Richard Ingram assumed the role of acting headmaster in early 1972. Following a visit to the academy campus in January 1972, Berry vice-president Milton McDonald commended new headmaster Ingram on the high morale of the students.[243]

Ingram and the students would be sorely tested when Hamrick Hall, the main classroom building at the academy, burned to the ground on February 21, 1972. The building was a total loss, and classes were cancelled for two days while Ingram and the faculty organized temporary classroom space in the basement of Friendship Hall. A mere four days following the fire, McDonald presented a report to the executive committee of the board of trustees on the future of the academy. Among the options considered were "(1) Phasing out the academy as rapidly as possible, (2) Relocation of the academy in the Ford Buildings, (3) Construction of a new building to replace Hamrick Hall and continuation of the academy in the present location and (4) Relocation of academy boys in Morton-Lemley Hall and the academy instructional program in the Ford Buildings." After much deliberation, the committee recommended that Hamrick Hall be rebuilt at its present site. A discussion was also held about adding grades six, seven and eight to the academy and adding female boarding students at some future date.[244]

What momentarily seemed like a devastating blow to the academy seemed to galvanize the faculty and students. "A major building is temporarily lost," said Ingram, "but the school is still very much alive. I have never been privileged to work with a more resourceful and resilient student body and faculty."[245] At the next chapel session, Chaplain August de Berdt called on the students to "work with your teachers because you are able to work closer than ever with them. Keep that creativity in your studying day after day... this is a call for you to rise up out of the ashes of the past into a new world which is yours."[246]

Much as their predecessors had done when the classroom building burned in 1955, the students and faculty pulled together and finished the school year in the close confines of the basement of Friendship Hall. As construction began on Hamrick Hall, the administration decided to go ahead with plans to add a middle school (grades six, seven and eight) to the academy with a basic curriculum that was "compatible with Berry's established college preparatory program." The school promised small classes and individual attention for students with classes held in Friendship Hall.[247] Leonard Diprima, a twelve-year-old student at the Elm Street School, was the first student to apply and be accepted at the new middle school. By the beginning of the 1972–73 school year, twenty-three students had been accepted into the middle school.

Plans to use Friendship Hall for middle school classes were derailed, however, when construction of Hamrick Hall fell behind schedule. The school year began with the high school students in the basement of Friendship and the middle school students making do in three training rooms in the Keown gymnasium that were temporarily converted into classrooms. Upon the completion of Hamrick Hall in January 1973, high school classes moved into the new building, and the middle school students moved into the Friendship Hall classrooms that had been used by the high school students for the past year.

Reflecting on the year just past, yearbook editor Tom Spector wrote,

Not unlike the phoenix, the building was rebuilt on its ashes into the most modern classroom facility we have known. At that point, Berry Academy left behind those troubled years which every institution must face at some time during its history. On the tightrope no longer, Berry was a progressive school with a bright future. Throughout the school, change was occurring, changes affecting all facets of the school and creating a general excitement in the school as a whole. We became interested in the future of our school, its directions, its changes.[248]

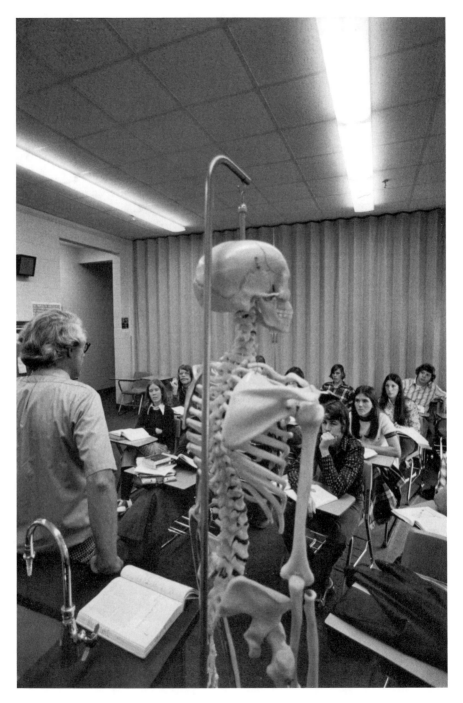

Gary McKnight's science class in the reconstructed Hamrick Hall, 1974.

Spector's optimism seemed apropos. Enrollment had increased more than 30 percent over the previous year at a time when private, independent schools across the country were contracting or closing at an alarming rate. Just weeks before the fire that destroyed Hamrick Hall, *Newsweek* magazine published an article entitled "Can Prep Schools Survive?" which declared that most of the nation's thousand or so independent secondary schools were "fighting for their very survival," and more than two dozen such schools had closed in the past four years.[249] But Berry Academy, it seemed, had weathered the storm, surviving the change from a work school for poor boys to a coeducational, college preparatory school with an associated middle school that promised to send more well-prepared students to the high school. And now the school had a new building that was one of the best classrooms on the Berry campus. The future did indeed seem bright at the end of the 1973 school year. But a tumultuous decade lay ahead.

Chapter 9

THE ENDING OF AN ERA

Change is a process, not an event.
—William P. Scheel

In less than a decade, the high school on the Berry mountain campus had transitioned from a boarding school dedicated to providing an educational opportunity for underprivileged boys to a coeducational, college preparatory school with an affiliated middle school. The changes had been dramatic and rapid. By 1972, day students made up half of the school's enrollment at the high school level. In an attempt to utilize the dormitory facilities more efficiently, the academy began accepting female boarding students for grades ten to twelve for the 1973–74 school year. Enrollment of male boarding students had declined to a level that could be accommodated in Pilgrim Hall, so plans were made to refurbish the upper floor of Friendship Hall, which had been the domain of senior boys, for the 24 boarding girls who would arrive in the fall of 1973. Enrollment during the 1972–73 school year was 195, and for the 1973–74 school year it reached 213, including 27 students in the middle school. Although the majority (97) of the high school students were commuters in the fall of 1973, the increase in enrollment for the third straight year was an encouraging sign following the struggles that the school had endured in the late 1960s, when enrollment had dropped to barely more than 100 students.

In spite of the enrollment uptick, many of the problems that had long plagued the school continued. In the spring of 1972, following the receipt

Academy students, including female boarding students, playing guitars, 1974.

of a petition signed by more than fifty students protesting regulations of male hair length, President Bertrand had announced that a two- to three-week moratorium on enforcing such regulations would be in place while a new Personal Appearance Committee made up of six students (including at least two girls), three faculty (including at least one woman), six parents (including three mothers and three fathers) and three members of the administration developed a new set of regulations regarding hair length and general appearance for the academy students. Bertrand clearly hoped that the females on the committee would have a moderating effect on the forthcoming recommendations. At the same time, Bertrand announced that Richard Ingram and Bill Thornton would assume the titles of headmaster and dean, respectively, effective during the summer. Ingram had arrived at Berry in 1970 to serve as dean of students and had become acting headmaster upon the departure of John Permenter in the middle of the 1971–72 school year. Thornton had come to Berry in 1968 as athletic director and had assumed the position of acting dean of students when Ingram became acting headmaster.

The Personal Appearance Committee wasted no time getting down to business. The parents group and the student group met independently to develop a list of suggested rules regarding hair length and clothing, and on April 19, 1972, the groups met with members of the administration to compare notes and develop a new personal appearance policy for the students. Consensus was quickly reached on clothing regulations—girls were not permitted to wear hot pants, backless tops, short shorts, tank tops, tie-dyed clothing or blue jeans, but they could wear walking shorts, pants or culottes. Boys could not wear tank tops, tie-dyed shirts or white T-shirts, but they could wear walking shorts, jeans and other casual pants and army clothing, provided it was neat, clean and properly sized. Shirts had to be tucked in, and everyone had to wear socks with any shoes that obviously required socks. The issue of hair length was more contentious. Several proposals were put forward, including a suggestion that there be no rule as to length as long as the hair was neat and clean, but the committee remained divided on the issue. Finally, admissions director Ed Laird took the floor and read the following statement:

> *From a philosophical and personal point of view, I favor no rule or regulation regarding dress or length of hair. I think it's nobody's business how you dress and wear your hair. Further, I believe anyone with a sense of history and a half-way open mind will not get upset by current fads and fashions and will be able to rise above their fears and prejudices which cause them to equate long hair with drugs or whatever their minds conjure up.*
>
> *But at the same time I realize that society outside the Berry Academy campus does not know us as individuals but judges us by first appearances and impressions. And since society around our campus is basically conservative, and since we cannot isolate ourselves like monks from the society, we must recognize and rationalize to some extent society's whims, fears, etc., however ludicrous, if for no other reason than for pure economics.*
>
> *Berry Academy's survival as an institution is to a large extent based on what people think of us, particularly local people since more and more of our students are coming from the local community. This will be even more true with the establishment of the new Middle School. If rumors reverberate through Floyd County that nobody but hippies and dope addicts attend Berry Academy, then we would stand to lose prestige, and consequently lose students and prospective students.*

Following this statement, Laird repeated his earlier motion that "the length of the hair be reviewed each year and that the length be determined by what is currently acceptable in the community, which is currently above the shoulders. It is further recommended that the hair must be neat, clean and either combed or brushed at all times." The second time around, Laird's motion passed overwhelmingly.[250]

While a review of the historical record indicates what may seem to be a disproportionate amount of time and energy being spent on the issue of hair length, Laird's statement and the events of the April 1972 Personal Appearance Committee meeting cut to the heart of what was perhaps the biggest issue for Berry Academy—that of public perception of the school and, consequently, the struggle to increase enrollment. Laird was not exaggerating when he said that the institution's survival depended on "what people think of us." In the early days of the school, Martha Berry had been a master of managing the public perception of her school and its students. Following her death, the image of the boys' school and its students began to change. By the time the board of trustees changed the name of the school to Berry Academy in 1964, the public image of the school was dramatically different. As former student Roark Summerford (65A) recalled, "It didn't take long to figure out that [Berry] was pretty rough...I didn't know you could even act like this." Summerford had transferred to Berry from a U.S. government school for the children of military families in Panama, where there was zero tolerance for bad behavior. He arrived at Berry Academy and for the first time witnessed students talking back to their teachers in class and cursing with impunity in the hallways. Academically, the school was behind what he had experienced in Panama as well. There was a perception that private schools were a place "where people sent discipline problems," recalled Summerford, and Berry was no different.[251] Although the administration had labored intensely to rehabilitate the image of Berry Academy, the image of the school as a second-tier private school that served as a dumping ground for students with disciplinary problems persisted.

Frank Campbell had fought mightily to change this perception during his tenure as headmaster, and Richard Ingram tried to carry forth with molding the school into a well-respected college preparatory institution. But the image of the high school was always burdened by the weight of its past. While the college had managed to move beyond its origins as a work-study institution for the poor and establish itself as a respectable liberal arts college, the academy still carried with it the image of being a school for students who had nowhere else to go, not because they had no money, but because they had either washed out or not been accepted at a more reputable institution. Although this image was a distortion of the reality at the academy, it was not entirely unfounded. Disciplinary problems persisted at the school. In a memo to the faculty, parents and students in November 1972, Headmaster Ingram outlined new policies regarding more structured study hall for dormitory students, including a supervised Saturday morning session for students with a grade-point average below 1.0 on the 4.0 scale, a stricter attendance policy that allowed for the suspension of a student who exceeded three unexcused absences in a quarter and a zero-tolerance policy for any student caught using illegal drugs or alcoholic beverages.[252]

According to John Shahan, a 1964 graduate of the MBSB who returned to the school in 1969 as the industrial arts instructor, illegal drugs began to become a problem at Berry Academy in the late 1960s. "Some of the kids then were actually sent to Berry because of those kinds of problems," said Shahan, adding, "The fact that there were day students made drugs and alcohol more available." The student body changed "from guys who had nothing to guys who had money," explained Shahan, and the presence of day students, who could come and go from the campus with greater freedom than the boarding students, meant that the boarding students had more opportunities to "escape" from the remote campus at the foot of Lavender Mountain. During his first three years as a teacher at Berry Academy, Shahan lived in one of the residence halls and served as a proctor. "I would smell pot every now and then," he recalled, "and I would see beer cans in the trash and the bushes," but catching the students in the act proved to be a difficult proposition. The arrival of girls on the campus dramatically changed the atmosphere, said Shahan, who characterized the tenure of Richard Ingram as a time when discipline was "lax." "We'd see kids walking off toward the hog farm or to the back of Swan Lake and wonder what they were up to. There really were no rules. The regulations didn't keep up with the changes in behavior," recalled Shahan. But the problems were not just a lack of discipline or failure to enforce the rules. "We had a different kind of student" during that time, according to Shahan.[253]

The apparent breakdown in discipline and ongoing problems associated with leadership at the academy led to a meeting of Bertrand, Ingram and representatives of the academy faculty in January 1974. The faculty evaluations of the school's position had just been completed, and Bertrand found cause for concern among the responses. In his opening remarks, Bertrand reviewed the history of the institution now known as Berry Academy, mentioned that Berry had its origins as a secondary school and noted that he had always been committed to the continued operation of the program in spite of repeated discussions over the years about discontinuing Berry's high school operation. On at least two occasions in the past eighteen years, most recently following the fire that destroyed Hamrick Hall, the board of trustees had seriously discussed discontinuing the academy; now, the school seemed to be at another crossroads. The group came to a consensus that the faculty was "not adequate in many areas" and that an administrative change at the academy was needed. While everyone agreed that Ingram was "a wonderful man and father," he had lost the confidence of the faculty and the students, and expecting him to continue as the headmaster under those circumstances "would be unfair to Ingram as well as the faculty and students." Ingram himself, in a great showing of magnanimity, agreed that what was best for Berry must be the top priority and left the room so that the faculty and the president would feel free to have an open and honest discussion about the future of the institution.[254]

The change in leadership at the academy came during the summer of 1974 with the arrival of Charles (Chuck) Johnston, who had previously served as the headmaster of the Brookstone School in Columbus, Georgia. Johnston seemed delighted to be on the picturesque Berry campus, exclaiming, "It's like living in the setting of a Walt Disney movie." He also promptly set about putting his own stamp on the school. He required students to have a full schedule of classes, six a day, eliminating the occasional free periods that many students had previously enjoyed during the school day. He explained that "the more intense academic program of a prep school is its main reason for being." He initiated a "sign-in and sign-out system" for boarding students that enabled the administration to keep close track of the students' whereabouts.[255] Johnston implemented a clan system aimed at increasing the sense of community within the school. Each student was assigned to one of six clans, each with a Scottish name such as MacArthur or MacDuff, and the clans became the basis for competition in intramurals, academic pursuits and service projects. Each clan had two faculty advisors. The hope was that the commingling of students, from freshmen to seniors, would create among them a bond that would transcend the usual class lines while creating a friendly rivalry among the clans. The clan system, which was met with some degree of skepticism by the students, was in place for two years before being abandoned as an organizing mechanism for school activities.

Johnston was "friendly with everybody," recalled former high school student Milton Chambers (78A), and his energy and enthusiasm provided a boost to morale on the campus. Much like his predecessors, he encountered formidable obstacles.[256] Following a series of meetings with the president and other administrative officials, Johnston summarized the problems facing the school and offered a plan of action for each point. Among the concerns were that new members of the faculty and staff were not "adequately educated to Berry's commitment to the work opportunity program," which Johnston still considered to be an important facet of Berry's program. Faculty and work supervisors needed more training in the history and purpose of the work program so that they could better mentor students in the value and satisfaction of "worthwhile work well done," according to Johnston. Related to the issue of the work program was the suggestion that every student be required to participate in some sort of work or service program for which they would receive no direct payment but rather credit toward their tuition, as had been done in the past at Berry.

The question of the maintenance and cleanliness of the campus and its facilities loomed large, and Johnston acknowledged that "student slovenliness" was an ongoing problem. Everyone on the campus needed to pitch in and help keep the campus and buildings "spotless" and less cluttered. Johnston also felt the high school was not effectively using its remarkable campus setting and recommended that more outdoor programs be developed, that the academy-college connection needed to be more fully exploited through the Joint Enrollment Program and that use of college facilities by the high school students be expanded. Perhaps of gravest concern was Johnston's observation that "a subtle erosion of a strict disciplinary framework may be occurring." The school was "understaffed for the number of students we are trying to inject with self-discipline," wrote Johnston, noting that thirty-six students had appeared before the discipline committee, all for serious rule infractions (drugs, alcohol, stealing, out of dorm at night, cutting classes). Eleven of those students had been asked to withdraw immediately, and another five were not invited back for the next school year.[257]

"The drug problem was rather rampant at the time," remembered Milton Chambers, who served as the chief justice of the disciplinary committee during his senior year. "We had a guy who every day would go out at lunch and smoke some dope and come back and lay his head down in class. Everybody just thought he was sleeping," said Chambers, who credited Coach Danny Farrar with keeping him on the straight and narrow path. "He had the greatest influence on me, Coach Farrar did, because I really like basketball. I think he singlehandedly kept me from trying drugs because everyone else in my senior class had at least tried drugs. There were maybe three of us that hadn't by the time we graduated."[258]

While trying to maintain discipline among the boys and girls who resided on campus proved to be a formidable challenge, there were outside forces that seemed to undermine the "security and well-being of Berry Academy" as well. In a memo to the committee of overseers of Berry Academy dated September 19, 1978, a group of faculty, parents and students expressed concern that the unfettered access to the campus granted to the public had led to serious concerns about the welfare of the students. The group cited incidents of beer cans being thrown at students from passing automobiles, unauthorized picnics on the lawns in areas that were purportedly off limits for picnicking, students from other schools observed smoking pot near the classroom building and in the woods near the reservoir and automobiles speeding down the Stretch road and around the buildings on the mountain campus. "The public has been allowed to take over the Berry campus to such an extent that many say it resembles a public park more than a private school," declared the group, adding that "its beauty is being destroyed by those who do not care and who do not contribute one farthing to Berry's present or future welfare." The group pleaded with the committee of overseers to help return Berry "to a quiet place of beauty and education," noting that "there must be a balance between unrestricted public use of the campus and complete isolation."[259]

Chuck Johnston remained at Berry Academy as the headmaster for two more years before departing to a position at the Trinity School in Atlanta. During Johnston's tenure, enrollment trended to upward of 200 students total in both the middle school and the high school. The ratio between day students and residential students at the high school, which had tipped significantly in favor of the day students in the mid-1970s, became more balanced with almost equal numbers in both categories throughout the later years of the decade. A major feature article in the *Rome News-Tribune* in March 1976 followed by a full-page advertisement in the August 1 issue of the newspaper likely helped boost enrollment, which grew from 184 in 1976 to 221 in 1977.[260] The renovation of the shop facilities adjacent to the Keown gymnasium in 1977 expanded the capacity of the middle school from 45 to 60 students.[261]

The construction associated with the expansion of the middle school, however, was an anomaly on the mountain campus. While the college had been the recipient of numerous gifts in recent years that allowed it to expand its infrastructure with new buildings (Hermann Hall, the new administration building that opened in 1964; Dana Hall, a new men's dormitory built in phases between 1959 and 1967; Krannert Center, a new student center that opened in 1969; and a major expansion of Memorial Library in 1976–77), the academy had received little in the way of funding for new buildings or improvements to its physical plant. In fact, the only new building constructed on the mountain campus during this flurry of building on the college campus was the reconstruction of Hamrick Hall following the fire in 1972. The academy, it seemed, had been relegated to secondary status from a development perspective. Repeated requests for improved student recreational facilities resulted in only modest efforts, such as the enclosure of the front porch of Hill Dining Hall and the addition of a pool table and a ping-pong table in the space. The athletic facilities at the academy remained far below what was deemed acceptable for a private college preparatory school that claimed to offer a well-rounded educational experience. Repeated requests from the headmaster for a new gymnasium or improvements to the existing facility were unsuccessful. The facilities at the Keown gymnasium were so inadequate that the high school basketball teams had to play all of their home games in the college gymnasium at the Ford Buildings.

The recession that gripped the nation throughout the mid-1970s squeezed the budgets at Berry, and for the most part, only building projects that were paid for by outside donors were carried out. No outside donors seemed especially interested in funding new facilities for the academy, so the school limped along with its aging physical plant. The setting remained bucolic, however, as noted by many of the students from the 1970s. Tom Fraker (76A) felt that "for someone like me who loves the outdoors, it couldn't have been a better location. I felt like I had tons of freedom, and just to have that much space to roam around in was great."[262] Mary Siceloff (76A), who came to Berry Academy after discovering that the public high school she was slated to attend in Atlanta led the state in shootings and rapes, remembered having a lot of freedom at the academy as well, and even though there was, on occasion, a sense of isolation, she loved the rural setting. "There was no gunfire," she exclaimed. "I really like being outside, and there was a lot of that here. I ran cross-country, and there were a lot of places to go."[263] The academy faced numerous difficulties, however, such as recurring budget shortfalls and the aforementioned disciplinary problems that continued to undermine the school.

The 1980–81 school year began with a new headmaster at the academy and a new president in charge of the Berry Schools. Dr. William Scheel arrived at Berry Academy during the summer of 1980 from Saint Mary's Hall–Doane Academy in New Jersey, where he served as headmaster for six years. Scheel's credentials were impressive, with a four-year stint as headmaster of Christchurch School in Christchurch, Virginia, prior to his time at Saint Mary's Hall–Doane Academy. He had been selected as a Ford Fellow while earning his EdD degree from the University of

Massachusetts–Amherst, and he also held a master of divinity degree and was an ordained priest in the Episcopal Church.[264] In January 1981, Scheel commented to *Lavender Blue* reporter Dan Tuck that he did not intend to bring "radical changes" to the academy, noting, "I like to think of change as a process, not an event," and that "any new administration brings some change in the way we do things and look at things."[265] Scheel arrived in time to oversee the long-overdue renovation of the academy's gymnasium, which took place during the 1980–81 school year. The project included a new roof and floor and the addition of a spectator gallery. Scheel was aware of the disciplinary problems at the academy, something he attributed to a combination of lax supervision and less-than-rigorous admissions standards. "The students at the academy were being treated like college students," he recalled. "They had almost no adult supervision, but they were fifteen and sixteen years old!" Rather than live in the headmaster's house, which was located at the end of the Stretch road, far removed from the dormitories, Scheel and his wife moved into an apartment at the end of Pilgrim Hall. Scheel was optimistic about his new job. President Gloria Shatto had said to him upon his arrival, "You can turn the academy around faster than I can change the college."[266]

Gloria Shatto began her tenure as president of the Berry Schools in January 1980. John Bertrand retired at the end of 1979 after almost twenty-four years as chief executive of the institution. Bertrand had struggled mightily in his first decade at Berry to redirect both the college and the high school, both of which had foundered in the decades after Martha Berry's death, but he had remained committed to carrying forward her vision into the second half of the century. An economist from Trinity University in San Antonio, Shatto had served on the board of trustees at Berry since 1975, so she was familiar with the school. Much as Bertrand had done before her, Shatto worked toward improving the image and reputation of the institution by strengthening the total program from its academic offerings and faculty to the work and religion-in-life programs.

Balancing the budget became a top priority, something Shatto focused on like a laser. The first six months of Shatto's tenure coincided with an economic recession, something that impacted Berry's investment portfolio and budget. The high school and college combined had a deficit of almost $300,000 for the 1979–80 fiscal year, and the 1980–81 budget forecast was for a deficit approaching $500,000. The board of trustees had in the past bridged the gap between income and expenses by tapping into the quasi-endowment, a category of the General Endowment Fund that the board of trustees had previously allocated as part of the endowment "with the right at a future date for use for current or capital purposes."[267] Of particular note was the need to supplement funding for the academy operations, which routinely exceeded 50 percent of the academy's annual budget.

Although enrollment at the academy generally increased between 1976 and 1980 (from 184 in 1976 to 223 in 1980), the net funding that the school was required to provide to cover the cost of operations beyond the income received through tuition and fees averaged almost $1,700 per student during that same period of time, peaking at $2,056 in 1980. The Academy Committee of Overseers, which met three times a year in advance of board of trustees meetings, wrestled with such problems as the public image of the school, the academic program and the aging physical plant at the mountain campus. At the October 8, 1980 meeting, Headmaster Scheel reported that "the previous administration had 'cleaned house' in the boarding department by not issuing reenrollment invitations to a number of troublesome students." According to Scheel, the house cleaning and a more selective admissions policy "had a salient effect on the quality of our student body and the tone of the school," and he anticipated a lower attrition rate in the coming year. Committee member Mitch Elrod noted that "the academy's image is not the best, due to past disciplinary and academic 'problems.'" Consequently, the school had failed to meet its enrollment targets for several years, especially for male residential students.[268]

In February 1981, the board of trustees voted to change the name of the institution from the Berry Schools to Berry College, Inc., a decision that raised eyebrows throughout the leadership at the academy. During the July and October board meetings, the future of the academy became the subject of in-depth discussion. Everyone agreed that in order for the academy to remain viable, an intensive recruitment program was necessary, and the academic program would need to be improved. In October 1981, Inman Allen, chair of the Academy Overseers Committee, stated that "the mission of the academy requires study by the Board of Trustees." Discussions ensued about completely revamping the school or possibly closing it altogether. Headmaster Scheel reported that enrollment for the 1981–82 school year was slightly over the previous year and that all efforts, including reducing staff, were being employed to control costs. Nevertheless, the academy had operated at a deficit of almost $500,000 the previous year.[269]

A list of reasons for discontinuing Berry Academy was presented to the board at the October meeting. The list was broken into four categories—financial, competition, image and overall deficit. The financial considerations included the need to supplement the high school operations at a level of around $475,000 a year, the inefficiency of the size of the school and pending major renovations to the boys' dormitory and the sewer system. Competition considerations included the superior image of the Darlington School, which seemed to dominate the private school market in the Rome–Floyd County area, the new Armuchee High School and the projected lack of population growth in the Rome area for the next twenty years. The academy also had an "image as [a] 'loser' in competitive events," which purportedly made recruiting difficult for Berry College, and the leadership of the public schools resented "Berry's efforts to recruit their best students for the Academy." Finally, the overall deficit, which Berry had been running since 1966, made fundraising from major foundations difficult. Board chairman William Bowdoin endorsed Allen's suggestion that an in-depth investigation of the academy's operations continue.[270]

Throughout the remainder of the 1981–82 school year, Scheel and the academy leadership worked tirelessly to address the questions and concerns of the board. A marketing plan for the school was developed that included a new brochure, a slide show and a series of recruiting events. The overseers agreed that the "type of student desired at the academy" needed to be more well defined.[271] The recruitment efforts bore little fruit, however. Although enrollment at the middle school for the fall of 1982 was 62 students in grades five through eight, the high school experienced a 20 percent drop in enrollment from 178 the previous year to 143.[272]

Just prior to the May 1982 board of trustees meeting, Berry College dean Doyle Mathis and executive assistant to the president Robert Lattimore asked local attorney James Maddox to consider the legal implications of closing the academy at the end of the 1981–82 school year. Maddox responded with a letter to President Shatto in which he acknowledged that the board of trustees was empowered by the institution's bylaws to decide whether any unit of the corporation should be "discontinued, modified, or expanded" but noted that there were several contractual issues related to the faculty and staff that might be problematic for Berry College, Inc. Most significantly, the school had extended contracts to the faculty and staff of Berry Academy in March and April, and most of the contracts had been accepted and returned. At the time the contracts were offered to academy personnel, "Berry College, Inc., knew the academy was being operated at a substantial loss"; consequently, wrote Maddox, the institution "could not rely on the claim of financial exigency to terminate the contract" of each faculty and staff member. Closing the academy at the end of the 1981–82 school year would leave Berry College, Inc., vulnerable to lawsuits from the faculty and staff for breach of contract, according to Maddox.[273]

Maddox's letter to Shatto, which was reviewed by the executive committee of the board of trustees at its May 25 meeting, convinced the committee to delay a decision on the future of the academy. At the same meeting, controller Joe Walton announced that the deficit for the current fiscal year had increased from $504,765 to a projected $835,000. Almost half of that amount, $398,780, was attributed to the academy's operations. The deficit would be covered from the school's real estate reserves and its quasi-endowment.[274] During the summer of 1982, Shatto and Controller Joe Walton both transferred their children from the academy to Darlington School, a move that contributed to a swirl of rumors that the academy was going to be closed. Both Shatto and Walton assured Scheel and other members of the Academy Overseers Committee that they had no plans to close the school.[275]

At the next meeting of the executive committee in September 1982, Walton informed the committee that lower-than-expected enrollment at the academy (205 students instead of the anticipated 240) meant that the academy's deficit for the 1982–83 fiscal year was expected to exceed $477,000. After review of data on the finances and enrollment at the academy, a motion, which was unanimously approved, was made "that the Executive Committee recommend to the Board of Trustees that Berry Academy be closed at the end of the 1982–83 school year."[276]

Seven days later, the Academy Overseers Committee held its regularly scheduled meeting in advance of the upcoming October board of trustees meeting. Several members of the executive committee who were present at the September 22 meeting of that body were also in attendance at the overseers meeting, but no mention was made of the unanimous recommendation by the executive committee to close the academy. Earlene Doster, the director of the middle school, gave a report on the growth and development of the middle school and the need for additional space to accommodate the present and future expected enrollment of the school. The quality of the middle school students had improved even as the number of students had increased in the past three years. Headmaster Scheel presented his report to the committee and noted that "in spite of some heavy concern in the community, with rumors flying all summer that the academy was going to close, we have maintained our day-student population—and the middle school has increased from 55 last year to 63."[277]

Scheel acknowledged that enrollment of boarding students was down, but he attributed the decline to the school's decision to adhere to its admission standards and not admit any student who was deemed "either socially or academically questionable" and "to accept only students who could adjust to our kind of residential life and who could do our academic work." According to Scheel, the academy could have had a "full house" for the 1982–83 school year but chose not to do so. Scheel spoke highly of new admissions director James Vaught, of whom he expected great things. "While a prediction at this point would be foolhardy," said Scheel, "I would almost be willing to wager a month's pay that next September will see a full house." Scheel reported on the austerity measures that he had implemented at the academy in an effort to save money and mentioned that renovations of the locker rooms at the academy gymnasiums, a project that was partially funded by money earned over several years by the parents club through the annual Berry Patch arts and crafts festival, had begun in late August. "In summary," concluded Scheel, "the school year has begun well. There is a stronger faculty, a better and happier student body and a positive feeling in the academy that has not existed in my previous two years as headmaster. The year promises to be a good one, and, barring financial disaster, the future appears bright."[278]

What is astonishing about the record of this meeting is the absence of any discussion about the possibility of closing the academy. In fact, the September 29, 1982 meeting of the overseers is one of the few meetings in which there was no serious discussion about discontinuing the academy operations. In a letter to trustee Inman Allen in January 1983, overseer Cecil Wright mentioned that he and other members of the committee were asked on September 29 "to do everything they could to help stop the rumors of the Academy's closing," leading Wright and other members of the committee to believe that the future of the school was indeed bright. Wright felt that he and other members of the overseers committee had been misled and betrayed.[279]

The next meeting of the board of trustees took place on October 16, 1982. At the end of the meeting, Bernard Storey moved that the trustees approve the recommendations of the executive committee, the last of which was that Berry Academy be closed at the end of the current school year.[280] A detailed plan was made for announcing the closure in mid-December shortly before Christmas break. Headmaster Scheel, admissions director James Vaught and other members of Shatto's executive team were summoned to a meeting in the boardroom of Hermann Hall shortly after the board meeting and were informed that the academy would be closed at the end of the current school year. Shatto forbade everyone in attendance from discussing the decision with anyone outside the room, including their families. Any such discussion would result in immediate termination. Scheel and Vaught returned to the mountain campus in a state of shock. Several nights later, they took a walk around the campus, and both agreed that they had to tell their wives what was happening. "The secrecy was unbearable," recalled Scheel. "We couldn't live like that." They both told their wives, swearing them to secrecy until the official announcement was made almost two months later.[281]

On Monday, December 13, letters from Scheel, board chairman William Bowdoin and alumni association president Percy Marchman were mailed to a variety of constituencies, including Berry alumni other than those who had a Mount Berry mailing address, academy parents, members of the board of trustees and the board of visitors, local city and county school superintendents, placement agencies and a list of special friends from the development office. That afternoon at 3:30 p.m., Shatto, Scheel, Joe Walton, Vaught and Chaplain Larry Green met with the academy faculty and staff at Barstow Library. Each attendee was handed a copy of the Bowdoin and Scheel letters, along with a transition services booklet. On Tuesday, December 14, Shatto and Scheel had breakfast with the non-trustee members of the Academy Committee of Overseers and the officers of the Berry Academy Parents Club. That same day, copies of the letters were sent out to on-campus alumni, as well as to college faculty and staff, through the on-campus mail system. The Rome media were alerted that a press conference would be held on Wednesday at 9:00 a.m. As might be expected, the local newspaper got wind of the announcement prior to the official press conference on December 15. The headlines in the *Rome News-Tribune* on December 14 read, "Berry to cease operations at Academy." The article, which cited "declining enrollment and rising costs" as the reasons for the closure, quoting Marchman's and Bowdoin's letters and adding that Berry officials had not been available for comment.[282]

Bowdoin's letter, which was addressed to all Berry Academy parents, students, faculty, staff and alumni, began with the statement that "when the forerunner of Berry Academy and Berry College began, there were only five public high schools in Georgia...Martha Berry and the Board of Trustees chose a course of decision, courage and progress. The board continued that tradition," wrote Bowdoin, noting that "Berry must use its resources most wisely in carrying out its mission today—meeting the educational requirements of changing times." The board had "reached a necessary but painful decision to close Berry Academy (grades five through twelve) at the end of the school year in June 1983," continued Bowdoin, adding that "the original purpose of Berry Academy has long ago been met." Bowdoin provided further context for the closing, citing the closing of the Martha

Berry School for Girls and the Possum Trot School as precedents for how the institution had adapted to changing times in the past. The recurring budget deficits were mentioned, including the requirement of $477,000 from the endowment for the current year and the decline in enrollment for the 1982–83 school year. The student work program was also not what it used to be, according to Bowdoin, since federal regulations limited participation in the program to older students. Furthermore, "college preparatory opportunities abound[ed] in both public and private schools" in the Rome area. Bowdoin promised that the final year of operation for the academy would be "complete and strong" and that transition assistance for both students and faculty and staff would be forthcoming.[283]

Alumni president Percy Marchman echoed Bowdoin's sentiments, reminding alumni that "Miss Martha Berry founded Berry to meet a specific need....As the needs of this region and its people changed over the years, Miss Berry changed the school to meet new needs." Marchman recounted the austerity measures that Berry had undertaken in recent years in an effort to balance the budget but noted that "falling enrollments and rising costs" at the academy made continuation of the high school imprudent. Noting that the decision was a painful one for the board, Marchman acknowledged that "for many, closing the Academy will be like losing a homeplace." Marchman suggested that "a distinguishing quality of Berry alumni is that they identify with Berry—not just the Academy, or high school or College. They are committed to the ideals and principles upon which Miss Berry founded and built her school." Marchman concluded that the alumni should "be grateful the best things about Berry continue—the good quality of faculty and staff and students, the respect for traditions and our heritage, and the reverence for the great mission that is Berry's alone—to educate the head, the heart and the hand in the spirit of service to others."[284]

In spite of the rumors that had run rampant throughout the summer that the academy might close, most of the students, parents, faculty, staff and alumni were stunned by the news. The announcement, made three days before academy students were released for winter break, was timed to minimize the opportunity for an immediate backlash from the on-campus community. The backlash might have been delayed, but it was forthcoming from a variety of sources.

Among those who responded to the news was former headmaster Fred Loveday, who was then serving as the executive secretary to the Georgia Association of Independent Schools. In a letter to Shatto dated January 13, 1983, Loveday stated that he regretted the decision to close Berry

Academy and that he also regretted "that there was no opportunity for dialogue before the decision was made." He enclosed with his letter an eight-page proposal for the continuation of Berry Academy. The academy, suggested Loveday, should become a "separate independent institution" complete with its own charter, endowment, board of trustees and reasonable acreage to permit the operation of the school. "For too long, the Academy has had to operate in the shadow of Berry College," wrote Loveday, adding that "historically, Berry Academy (under a different name in earlier years) is the parent institution of The Berry Schools," although it had been "relegated to step-child category" in the years since Martha Berry's death, according to Loveday. He took issue with Bowdoin's claim that the development of a more robust public school system should mean the demise of a private school like Berry Academy, stating that "the noble and distinctive ideas and ideals that brought Berry into existence must be perpetuated as a sacred mission." Loveday acknowledged that it was time for change at the academy, but he argued that the change should be something that would breathe new life into the institution, not terminate it. Loveday had "no doubt whatsoever that the closing of Berry Academy would be a violation of the visions of Martha Berry," a claim that many high school alumni would echo for years to come.[285]

The Berry Academy Parents Club responded with equal fervor, stating that "we do not, at this point, based on the information that has been presented, accept the decision that the Academy should be closed. We do not believe that such a closing is in the best interest of Berry. If, however, we are not correct in our judgment and the Academy must be closed, then it must be closed in a more honest, forthright manner than what we have witnessed to date." The "lack of honesty" surrounding the way in which the decision was made and the delay in the dissemination of the decision was a major point of contention for the members of the parents club, who also did not accept "declining enrollment" and "budget deficits" as viable reasons for closing the school. Noting that the middle school's enrollment was at an all-time high and that the drop in enrollment for the high school reflected the imposition of stricter admissions standards, the parents argued that using the declining-enrollment argument represented a great deception on the part of the administration. The parents were especially angry that money raised through their efforts at the Berry Patch was spent on improvements at the academy gym after the administration knew it would be closing the school. Perhaps most egregious was the "deception regarding the closing plans." The parents claimed that Shatto's sons, who had transferred from Berry

Academy to Darlington prior to the beginning of the school year, had told other students during the 1981–82 school year "that their mother intended to close the Academy." Rumors to that effect had swirled throughout the Rome area throughout 1982, and each time the question was raised, Shatto and other members of the leadership offered assurances that the school would not be closed.[286]

The parents club refused to accept defeat and drafted a proposal to the board of trustees to keep the academy open. Three members of the club met with the executive committee of the board on January 14 to present their proposal, which included a plan for reducing the amount of supplemental funding required by the academy by more than half a million dollars through increased enrollment and an aggressive fundraising program. The plan included Loveday's idea that the academy become a separate and independent entity with a portion of the current endowment signed over for use by Berry Academy.[287] A letter from board chairman Bowdoin on January 27 announced that the executive committee had considered the proposal but had "concluded regrettably there is no truly realistic possibility of obtaining the additional funding suggested." Bowdoin defended President Shatto, who had become a target of much anger and derision in the wake of the announcement of the academy's closing, and stated that the decision was not prompted by Shatto but was one made by the board after "careful consideration of the operation of the academy." Bowdoin further stated that the board's decision to change the corporate name from the Berry Schools to Berry College, Inc., which had been controversial in its own right, had been his idea.[288]

After meeting with the executive committee, the president of the parents club, William Irmscher, stated that "based on the facts that the Trustees had to work with, any objective businessman would have voted to close the Academy."[289] But some of the parents were not ready to give up. In mid-February, a $1.78 million lawsuit was filed on behalf of John D. Jackson and the parents of about two hundred students against the members of the board of trustees and President Shatto. The suit alleged that "the individual members of the Board of Trustees in acting in a fraudulent manner in their relationship with the Plaintiffs, have violated their trust and their obligation to Berry College, Inc." The defendants were charged with "five different counts, including negligence; willful negligence; fraud and deceit; breach of contract; and one count for the removal of the trustees from the board of the corporation."[290] Jackson's suit was dismissed by Judge Robert Walther, as were two additional lawsuits filed by parents of academy students in 1984.[291]

Debate about the necessity of closing the academy would divide much of the Berry alumni community for years to come. While many alumni and members of the Berry community could never accept that closing the academy was necessary, others felt that the move was a logical progression for the institution. Alumnus Roark Summerford (65A) recalled that the "school was hanging on by its fingernails when we were there" in the 1960s.[292] John Shahan (64A), who was both an alumnus of the school and a former faculty member, felt that "the time had come" for the school to close.[293]

Many of those who agreed with the decision took issue with its timing and execution. The sentiment felt by many members of the community in the weeks and months after the announcement of the closing is perhaps best captured in the letter from academy overseer Cecil Wright to trustee Inman Allen, written in January 1983, in which Wright compares being "blind-sided" by those whom he considered to be "friends and teammates" to the ambush by the Japanese at Pearl Harbor on December 7, 1941. Wright recounted how he had served for six years on the Academy Overseers Committee, all the while believing in the mission of the school and publicly defending the institution. He acknowledged that the board had the right to make the decision to close the academy, but he took issue with the way in which the decision was made, citing the administration's decision to allow the parents club to spend $22,000 of their own money on repairs to the gymnasium after the decision to close the school had already been made, as well as the years of neglect to which the facilities at the academy had been subjected. According to Wright, "The academy was not given a fair chance," and to add insult to injury, the faculty and the committee of overseers "found out the academy was closing just hours before the local newspaper ran a story on it." The overseers "were seeing a bright light at the end of the tunnel in student population quality and numbers," according to Wright, only to have their hopes dashed by what seemed to be a snap decision that had been made behind closed doors with no involvement of the overseers, the parents, alumni or friends. Had appeals to those groups been made, and had the efforts to right the ship failed, "then we would have been satisfied knowing that we had done all that could be done, and closing the doors would be the only choice," wrote Wright.[294]

The last graduation at the mountain campus was held on Saturday, June 4, 1983. According to *Rome News-Tribune* staff writer David Royal, "The joy was less vibrant as the Class of '83, the final graduating class at Berry Academy, went through commencement exercises at Frost Chapel." The ceremony was "tinged by the awareness that part of a 'living monument' to Martha Berry is being put to rest." About 20 percent of the students had dropped out of the school following the announcement, leaving only 165 students remaining at year's end. Graduating senior David Bachler lamented the closing, saying, "I always thought I'd have a place to come back to....Now there's a sense of my roots having been pulled up." Longtime teacher and coach Gary McKnight commented, "This school has been a beacon in this state," adding that he felt as if "some ideas are being snuffed out." Describing the final months of the school year, one teacher stated, "It was like a wake that went on for months and months." McKnight, who had been at Berry Academy for more than twenty years, was forced to look for another job, something "he was not very good at," he realized, as he had not been on the job market for more than two decades.[295] However, he was one of the lucky ones who did find employment at another private school. Not everyone was so lucky. Headmaster Scheel had spent the last six months of the school year helping the faculty find jobs, but he himself had no prospects when the school year ended. "My career was in ruins," he recalled, noting that it would have been difficult to find a headmaster's job after having the academy close under his watch. Much like the captain of a sinking ship, Scheel closed down the academy, remaining in his Pilgrim Hall apartment until early August. Unable to find another suitable job in the education field, Scheel and his wife left to spend a year in England with his wife's family. He eventually returned to the States and began working for the Association of Episcopal Schools.[296]

In spite of the fact that discussions about discontinuing the high school at Berry had been going on for forty years, the suddenness with which the closing happened was startling. Because the decision to close the academy, which Fred Loveday described as the "parent institution of the Berry Schools," was made behind closed doors with little or no community involvement, it seemed unreasonable, unfair and duplicitous. History would prove that the board made a sound financial decision. The endowment of Berry College, Inc., which hovered around $22 million in 1982, had grown to more than $760 million by September 2011.[297] However, the emotional cost to the people to whom the school had meant so much was incalculable.

Epilogue

We are standing on holy ground.
—Jeannette Cathy

In the weeks and months following the announcement of the closing of Berry Academy, rumors about possible uses for the facilities on the mountain campus ran rampant. The April Fools edition of the on-campus newspaper for Berry College announced that the academy campus would be converted into a nudist colony under the name of Lavender Mountain Nudist Colony, Inc. The paper reported that a fictitious board chairman proclaimed the move was "immoral but profitable" and that "it was high time this institution got hip and moved into the '60s."[298] Two weeks later, vice-president of resources John Lipscomb, who was the college's spokesman regarding potential uses for the facilities, announced that the school had received a number of inquiries about possible uses of the campus that could be narrowed down into a few categories. The first type was a "school with a different slant," such as a state-funded school for gifted students that focused on special fields of study. The second option under consideration was converting the campus into a conference and continuing education center that could be used by Berry and other schools. Other options were a training/conference center operated by a private company or a retirement village that would "be a means for people formerly connected to Berry to return here and in a learning situation—to live, learn, and work at Berry again."[299]

At its February 18, 1983, meeting, the board of trustees approved the following "tentative conditions and criteria for the use of the academy facilities:

1. Use and personnel involved must be compatible with Berry College and its mission.

2. Reimbursed use by an outside agency is favored over an activity created by Berry.

3. Management by an outside agency is favored over operation by Berry.

4. Income to Berry should, as a minimum, cover the cost of all services and maintenance provided by Berry.

5. A use that would involve college faculty, staff and students on a mutually beneficial basis is favored.

6. The facilities are not for sale.[300]

By mid-summer, more than a half dozen interested parties had toured the campus, ranging from a retirement home group affiliated with the United Methodist Church to a Saudi Arabian prince. Lipscomb acknowledged that the prince had visited the campus to study the architecture and landscape of Berry, but he denied that the prince had any interest in acquiring the campus. The campus was "available for educational and humanitarian uses determined appropriate by the board of trustees," Lipscomb stated, but he reiterated that it was not for sale.[301]

At the October 15, 1983 meeting of the board, President Shatto presented comments regarding the challenges faced by Berry—from keeping tuition affordable to ending seventeen years of operating deficits. She noted that private colleges, especially small institutions like Berry, faced formidable obstacles at a time when the vast majority of students were enrolled in public institutions. More than one hundred colleges and universities had closed in the past decade, reported Shatto, largely because they were "educationally weak, badly managed, with small or nonexistent endowments, and those endowments have declined because they have continuing operating deficits." Shatto was determined that Berry College would not be among the hundreds of private colleges forced to close in the coming decades. She pointed out that Berry College had a unique mission, a powerful board of trustees, strong alumni support and good-quality students, faculty, staff and alumni. "Berry people have the imagination, the will and the spirit to assure that Berry will not simply survive, but will flourish," Shatto concluded.[302]

In early October 1984, controller Joe Walton announced that "for the first time in 17 years, Berry College was able to balance the fiscal budget for current operations, without applying any unrestricted bequests." For many years, the school had been expending the quasi-endowment funds just to make ends meet. Finally, through what Walton described as "a rather long process which was achieved by getting a better return on revenue-producing resources of Berry, tighter control of expenditures, and by cutting some of the programs," the school was on track to build rather than spend its endowment. Walton noted that "last year was the first full year of operation without the academy," citing that as a factor that contributed to the balanced budget.[303]

The academy facilities on the mountain campus sat empty for the 1983–84 school year, but in the summer of 1983, serious discussions about a potential use for the facilities began with Chick-fil-A founder Truett Cathy. At an event in Atlanta, Gloria Shatto approached Cathy, who had previously visited Berry, about the possibility of Chick-fil-A's using the former academy facilities, and initially Cathy declined. Following his conversation with Shatto, Cathy had an epiphany. He and his wife, Jeannette, traveled to Berry, where they were given a tour of the shuttered dormitories and dining hall. As they were preparing to leave the mountain campus, Cathy opened the door for his wife and asked, "What do you think?"

"We're standing on holy ground," she replied.

That day, recounted WinShape Foundation director Bob Skelton, Berry College and Chick-fil-A determined that they would co-sponsor a scholarship program for students who had worked at Chick-fil-A during high school.[304] Cathy created the WinShape Foundation based on "his desire to 'shape winners' by helping young people succeed in life through scholarships and other youth."[305] Berry and the WinShape Foundation formalized an agreement in January 1984 that provided for scholarship support from the foundation and additional financial aid from Berry through its general fund and its work program to allow "Chick-fil-A scholars" to attend Berry College.[306]

When classes began at Berry College in the fall of 1984, the two dormitories at the mountain campus each housed thirty-four students. College women lived in Friendship Hall, and the men lived in Pilgrim Hall. Since that time, WinShape has expanded its operations on the mountain campus to include summer camps for boys and girls, a retreat in the former Normandy dairy complex and several foster homes. In 1987, Hamrick Hall, the former high school classroom building, became the home for the Berry Elementary School, a program for kindergarten through fifth grade that had begun in 1977 as the Early Learning Center.

Truett Cathy, founder of Chick-fil-A.

The WinShape Foundation sign, which replaced the Berry Academy Falcons sign in 1984. *Author's collection.*

The former high school classroom building, Hamrick Hall, now serves as the Berry College Elementary School. *Author's collection.*

While many alumni of the high school were at first wary of the Berry/Chick-fil-A alliance, most of them have come to appreciate the corporation's support of Berry College. As John Shahan explained, "They've carried on Martha Berry's mission, just in a different way."[307] Recalling the great impact that his time at the MBSB had on his life, Luke Lamb (64A) stated, "It helped mold me as a person to appreciate hard work and to have compassion." When asked about the closing of the school, Lamb responded, "We would all like to see the school be as it was, but at least it's still available. It's been a blessing."[308] Alumnus Stewart Fuqua (80A), who has returned to Berry College every year since 1998 to participate in the Alumni Work Week program, reflected fondly on his time at the academy. "I wouldn't trade anything for my experience here," he said, but "if you couldn't make the economics work, then closing made sense. It's been a blessing that Truett Cathy came along. There might be nothing left if he hadn't."[309]

As the date approached for my thirtieth high school reunion in 2007, I was interested to talk to my former classmates about their sentiments regarding our former school. Classmates of mine who had not been back to campus since they graduated came back for the occasion. When I inquired of one of them if she was angry that the academy had closed, she seemed startled. "I don't think about it like that," she said. "The buildings are still there. There are still students living in the dorms, and the place is alive. It's still a school, and that's what matters."[310]

Perhaps she is right. The mountain campus today is alive with college students and elementary school children throughout the school year and is filled with campers who participate in the WinShape Foundation summer camp programs during the summers. Alumni often comment that the WinShape program is a continuation of Martha Berry's mission of providing an education for students who might not otherwise be able to afford one. The school has evolved into a well-respected liberal arts college that is renowned for its work program and its beautiful campus, both of which are most impressive. But for those of us who spent our teenage years on the mountain campus, nothing will ever quite recapture the magic of our high school years at the base of Lavender Mountain. It is perhaps easier to romanticize our time there simply because the high school we attended no longer exists. Unbeknownst to those of us who were students there, the historical record shows that keeping the high school going was a long, difficult struggle. It is indeed a miracle that it survived as long as it did.

The school that ended its days as Berry Academy was the most direct descendant of Martha Berry's original school, something that gave it

The Stretch road that connects the mountain campus to the main campus, 2013. *Author's collection.*

special significance in the history of the institution. But for those of us who attended high school on the mountain campus, it was not the history that meant so much to us; rather, it was that "intangible magic" of the place where we worked and played and studied that we remember. We encountered mentors who shaped our lives and developed relationships that have lasted a lifetime. Its inglorious ending notwithstanding, Martha Berry's school on the mountain campus lives on in our memories.

Appendix A

IMPORTANT DATES IN THE HISTORY
OF THE HIGH SCHOOL

1902   Martha Berry establishes the Boys Industrial School on the lower campus.

1908   The school's name is legally changed to the Berry School.

1909   Martha Berry School for Girls opens on the log cabin campus.

1910   Former president Theodore Roosevelt visits the school.

1914   The First Mountain Day celebration is held at the base of Lavender Mountain.

1916   Mount Berry Farm School is established on the mountain campus with Grady Hamrick as principal.

1917   The name of the corporation is changed to the Berry Schools.

1922   Mount Berry Farm School becomes the Foundation School.

1926   Friendship Hall burns while under construction.

1926   Berry Junior College is established, and freshmen and sophomore high school boys are moved to the mountain campus.

1930   The mule barn and industrial shop adjacent to the gymnasium burn.

1930   Berry College is established, the remainder of high school boys are moved to the mountain campus, the Foundation School is discontinued and the high school's name is changed to the Mount Berry School for Boys.

1942   Martha Berry dies.

1947   Fred Loveday becomes principal of the Mount Berry School for Boys.

1955   The classroom building (later known as Hamrick Hall) burns.

1956   The Martha Berry School for Girls closes.

1957   A storage barn at the Normandy dairy complex burns.

1964   The Mount Berry School for Boys becomes Berry Academy.

1966   Fred Loveday resigns as headmaster of Berry Academy.

1966   Day students are admitted.

1968   The first African American student, Roy Lee Hunter, is admitted to Berry Academy.

1971   Girls are enrolled at Berry Academy as day students.

1972   The middle school (grades six to eight) opens at Berry Academy.

1973   Friendship Hall is converted to a girls' dorm to accommodate female boarding students.

1978   The Berry Schools are listed on the National Register of Historic Places as a nationally significant historic district.

1982   The institutional name is changed from the Berry Schools to Berry College, Inc.

1983   Berry Academy closes.

1984   Chick-fil-A agrees to a partnership with Berry College that involves the use of mountain campus dormitories, and the WinShape Centre is established.

1984   The WinShape Summer Camp program begins on the mountain campus.

2001   Chick-fil-A renovates the Normandy Barns to create the WinShape Retreat.

Appendix B

HIGH SCHOOL AND ACADEMY LEADERS
FROM 1916 TO 1983

Grady Hamrick, superintendent/principal, 1916–45
James Armour Lindsay, principal, 1946
Kenneth Moore, principal, 1946–47
Fred Loveday, principal, 1947–64, headmaster, 1964–66
Robert Crawford, headmaster, March 1966–June 1966
Frank Campbell, headmaster, July 1966–71
John Permenter, headmaster, 1971
Richard Ingram, headmaster, 1972–74
Chuck Johnston, headmaster, 1974–80
William Scheel, headmaster, 1980–83

Appendix C

LIST OF INTERVIEWS

John Franklin Adams (54H)

Larry B. Adams (56H, 60C)

Madison Alexander (51H)

Gene Anderson (63H)

Frances D. Barnett (49C)

Martha Bowen (55H)

Thomas A. Bowen (55H)

Tom Butler (65A)

William Milton Chambers (78A, 82C)

Jerry Chastain (65A)

John Chastain (62H)

Don Collins (65A)

Dale Cummings (66A)

Johnnie S. Curry (52H, 55C)

Tim Dixon (81A)

Ronald Edwards (56H)

John Donald Fite (51H)

Jimmy Fletcher (64A, 68C)

Lamar Fletcher (66A)

Tom Fraker (76A)

Stewart Fuqua (80A)

Randolph Green (37H, 41C)

Ruth Thomas Hale (38H)

James Hamrick (59H, 63C)

John K. Hamrick (43H, 47C)

Bernice Holcomb (56H)

John Jordin (65A)

Wilma Kenney (48H)

David Kirkland (75A)

Tim Knight (81A)

Luke Lamb (64h)

Luis Leon (67A)*

Betty Little (51H)

Wallace Lloyd (43H, 50C)

Olin McCarty (47H)

Ralph W. McDonald (46H)

Gary E. McKnight (61C, faculty)

Charles E. McLeod (54H)

Patsy H. McLeod (56H)

Virginia Mosby (52H)

Mike Murdock (73A)

Joan Kitchens Myers (50H, 54C)

Ron Pierce (60H)

Tom Poe (48H, 52C)

Harold Posey (56H)
Joseph Eugene Price (56H)
Art Pugh (52H, 56C)
Frances Richey-Goldby (83A, 87C)
William Scheel (faculty)*
Bill Segrest (48H, 51C)
John Shahan (64A, 69C)
Jerry W. Shelton (faculty)
Bennie W. Shipp (47H)
Mary Siceloff (76A)
Harold Sowell (56H)
Roark Summerford (65A)

Roger Sundy (53H)
Steve Tankersley (56H)
Brewster Turley (66A)
Edmond L. Underwood (43H)
Robert Webb (47H)
Willa White (48H)
Robert H. Williams (62H)
Jerry L. Winton (56H)
Harry Wise (57H)
Rosa Wright (47H, 51C)

H denotes graduate of the Mount Berry School for Boys or the Martha Berry School for Girls.

A denotes graduate of Berry Academy.

C denotes graduate of Berry College.

Lowercase indicates the person attended but did not graduate from the school.

*Telephone interview, no recording available. Notes in possession of the author.

All interviews are the property of Berry College and are available at the Berry College Archives unless otherwise noted.

NOTES

INTRODUCTION

1. William Kline, e-mail message to Tom Butler, May 25, 2010.
2. Ibid.
3. Jack Pigott, e-mail message to Tom Butler, May 23, 2010.
4. Board of Trustees Minutes, February 18, 1983.
5. Ibid., October 1983.

CHAPTER 1

6. *Rome Tribune*, "Industrial School for Boys," January 1, 1902.
7. *Rome Tribune*, "Most Worthy Institution," January 12, 1902, 12.
8. *Rome Tribune*, "Noble Work for Poor Boys," January 14, 1902, 4
9. *Atlanta Constitution*, "Noble Work of Miss Berry," January 18, 1902, 3.
10. James A. Hall, "Boys' Industrial Home of Floyd County, A Unique Success!," *Atlanta Constitution*, July 19, 1903, B6.
11. *Atlanta Constitution*, "Miss Berry is at the Head of an Unique Institution," January 3, 1904, B2.
12. *Atlanta Constitution*, "The Making of Georgia Manhood," April 24, 1906, 8.
13. Ibid.
14. *Atlanta Constitution*, "The Boys' Industrial School," January 28, 1907, 4.

15. John Corrigan Jr., "$100,000 Endowment Fund for Martha Berry School," *Atlanta Constitution*, May 12, 1909.

16. *Atlanta Constitution*, "How I Met Roosevelt," October 6, 1910, 6.

17. Theodore Roosevelt to Martha Berry, January 9, 1909, MB Collection.

18. Corrigan, "$100,000 Endowment Fund."

19. *Southern Highlander*, "For the Mountain Girls," June 1910, 81.

20. Ibid., 82.

21. John Corrigan Jr., "Conservation of Children Object of Berry School," *Atlanta Constitution*, October 11, 1910.

22. Kenneth Coleman, ed., *History of Georgia* (Athens: UGA Press, 1991), 240–41.

23. *Berry Schools Bulletin*, 1916–1917, 14.

Chapter 2

24. *Berry Alumni Quarterly*, "An Opportunity for Ten Boys to Earn an Education," November 1915, back cover.

25. S.H. Cook, *Half Century at Berry* (Mount Berry: Berry College, 1961), 67.

26. H.G. Hamrick, "The Mount Berry Farm School," *Southern Highlander*, 1922, 11.

27. Cook, *Half Century at Berry*, 25.

28. *Berry Schools Bulletin*, 1916–1917, 65–66.

29. Ibid., 11.

30. Ibid., 10–11.

31. Martha Berry to John Eagan, September 29, 1916, MB Collection.

32. Martha Berry to John Eagan, October 14, 1916, MB Collection.

33. Ibid.

34. *Berry School News*, September 26, 1916, 1.

35. W.F. Bradley, *Berry School News*, January 9, 1917, 4.

36. Martha Berry to John Eagan, December 29, 1916, MB Collection.

37. Martha Berry to John Eagan, January 5, 1917, MB Collection.

38. Ibid.

39. *Berry News*, "A Most Pleasant and Profitable Day is Spent at the Foundation School," October 24, 1923, 1.

40. Cook, *Half Century at Berry*, 25.

41. Martha Berry to Grady Hamrick, April 17, 1922, MB Collection.

42. Tracy Byers, *Glory of Young Manhood and Womanhood*, 70.

43. *Berry News*, "The Foundation School," September 14, 1922, 4.

44. *Berry News*, "Some Needs of the Berry Schools," October 5, 1922, 6.

45. *Berry News*, "Work at the Foundation School," October 31, 1922, 2.

46. *Berry News*, "A Talk Given by Miss Berry to the Students at Foundation School," October 31, 1922, 2.

47. *Berry News*, "Berry's 1923 Growth," September 18, 1923, 1.

48. *Berry News*, "Foundation School," October 24, 1923, 2.

49. *Berry News*, "Foundation School," October 24, 1923, 2.

50. Byers, *Glory of Young Manhood and Womanhood*, 121.

51. *Mount Berry News*, "Foundation School Grows by Leaps," March 22, 1924, 1.

52. *Mount Berry News*, "Remarkable Growth of Last Established Unit of the Schools," March 31, 1925, 1.

53. Martha Berry to Grady Hamrick, August 14, 1925, MB Collection.

54. *Mount Berry News*, "Dormitory Burns at Berry," May 5, 1926, 1.

55. *Mount Berry News*, "The Freshmen of the Foundation School," October 1, 1926, 3.

CHAPTER 3

56. *Mount Berry News*, "Junior College Courses Added," September 15, 1926, 1.

57. *Mount Berry News*, "Berry's New Era," September 15, 1927, 2.

58. *Mount Berry News*, "The Gymnasium," February 1, 1928, 4.

59. *Mount Berry News*, "As Seen from the Mountain," February 1, 1928, 3.

60. *Mount Berry News*, "Fire Destroys Dormitory at Farm School," January 6, 1930, 1.

61. *Mount Berry News*, "Shop and Barn at High School in $30,000 Fire," February 15, 1930, 1.

62. *Mount Berry News*, "New Shops at High are in Use Now," September 24, 1930, 1.

63. *Mount Berry News*, "2528 Teeth Filled by Dr. Rounds," April 15, 1931, 4.

64. *Mount Berry News*, "Water Mill at High," October 15, 1930, 3.

65. *Mount Berry News*, "Growth of Berry is Described by Visitor," November 1, 1930, 1.

66. *Mount Berry News*, "Study Habits of High Observed," February 2, 1931, 1.

67. Hamilton Basso, "About the Berry Schools," *New Republic*, April 4, 1934, 208.

68. Martha Berry to Grady Hamrick, September 19, 1933, MB Collection.

69. Edwin Holman, "Berry Schools Students Foil Attempts to Foment Strike," *Atlanta Constitution*, October 8, 1933.

70. Martha Berry to Emily Vanderbilt Hammond, October 11, 1933, MB Collection.

71. Don West to Leland Green, July 31, 1926.

72. *Berry Alumni Quarterly*, "Don West Achieves Fame as Poet," March 1932, 11.

73. Don West, "Sweatshops in the Schools," *New Republic*, October 4, 1933, 216.

74. *New Republic*, October 25, 1933, 292.

75. Martha Berry to Emily Vanderbilt Hammond, October 21, 1933, MB Collection.

76. Martha Berry to Emily Vanderbilt Hammond, October 28, 1933, MB Collection.

77. Martha Berry to Emily Vanderbilt Hammond, January 15, 1934, MB Collection.

78. Basso, "About the Berry Schools," 206.

79. Ibid., 208.

80. John Hamrick interview by Ouida Dickey, June 1, 2009.

81. Martha Berry to Grady Hamrick, April 10, 1933, MB Collection.

82. Martha Berry to Grady Hamrick, April 12, 1934, MB Collection.

83. *Mount Berry News*, "New Dairy Soon Ready," October 5, 1935, 4.

84. "The Reminiscences of M. Gordon Keown," Ford Motor Company Archives Oral History Section, 1952, 17.

85. *Mount Berry News*, "Frost Chapel to be Dedicated," October 11, 1937, 4.

86. *Mount Berry News*, "Boys Build Barstow Memorial," November 20, 1940, 4.

87. Evelyn Pendley, *Sixty Years of Education*, 13.

88. Ouida Dickey and Doyle Mathis, *Berry College: A History* (Athens: UGA Press, 2005), 80–81.

CHAPTER 4

89. *Southern Highlander*, "Miss Berry Provides for Future of Schools in Final Messages," Spring 1942, 7–8.

90. Dickey and Mathis, *Berry College*, 73, 81.

91. Victor Butterfield to John A. Sibley, April 28, 1942, 1, Sibley papers, Berry College Archives.

92. Ibid., 5.

93. Ibid., 4.

94. Ibid., 8.

95. Ibid., 9.

96. Philip Weltner to John A. Sibley, June 30, 1943, Sibley papers.

97. John A. Sibley to G. Lamar Westcott, July 14, 1943, Sibley papers.

98. G. Lamar Westcott to John A. Sibley, July 16, 1943, Sibley papers.

99. G. Lamar Westcott to John A. Sibley, July 21, 1943, Sibley papers.

100. Philip Weltner to Gordon Keown, August 12, 1943, 1, Sibley papers.

101. Gordon Keown to Philip Weltner, August 17, 1943, Sibley papers.

102. Philip Weltner to John A. Sibley, October 11, 1943, Sibley papers.

103. Philip Weltner, "To the Board of Trustees of the Berry Schools: A Report with Recommendations," October 1943, 1, Sibley papers

104. Ibid., 2.

105. Ibid., 3.

106. Ibid., 5.

107. Ibid., 7.

108. Ibid., 8.

109. Floyd County Board of Education, "Armuchee High School," http:// www.floydboe.net/fcshistory/MainHistory.cfm.

110. Weltner, "To the Board of Trustees," 13.

111. John A. Sibley to Philip Weltner, October 13, 1943, Sibley papers.

112. G. Lister Carlisle to John A. Sibley, November 4, 1943, Sibley papers.

113. Ralph McDonald interview by Ouida Dickey, June 4, 2009.

114. Bennie Shipp interview by Ouida Dickey, June 3, 2009.

115. Bob Kayler, MBSB Reunion Dinner, Mount Berry, Georgia, May 30, 2009.

116. William Segrest interview by Carolyn Smith, June 3, 2009.

117. Don Fite interview by Ouida Dickey, May 31, 2009.

118. Bob Kayler, speech at the Class of 1959 Reunion Dinner, Hill Dining Hall, Mount Berry, Georgia, 2009.

119. *Chattanooga Times*, "Recitation Hall at Berry Burned," November 29, 1955; *Mount Berry News*, "Fire Destroys H.S. Building," December 1955, 1.

120. *Mount Berry News*, "Activities Are Resumed in New High School Recitation Hall," January 1957, 1.

121. *Berry Alumni Quarterly*, October 1957.

Chapter 5

122. *Rome News Tribune*, "Berry President Points to New Role of School," September 4, 1956, 1.

123. John R. Bertrand, "Lines from the President's Desk," *Mount Berry News*, December 13, 1957, 2.

124. 1958 Educational Survey of The Berry Schools, JRB Collection, xvii.

125. Ibid., xviii.

126. Ibid., xix.

127. Ibid., xix–xx.

128. Ibid., 141.

129. Ibid., 142.

130. Ibid., 146.

131. Ibid., 149.

132. *The Berry Schools Bulletin*, 1955–56, 25, 75.

133. 1958 Educational Survey of the Berry Schools, 156.

134. Ibid., 164.

135. Art Pugh interview by Ouida Dickey, June 2, 2009.

136. Frank Adams interview by Ouida Dickey, June 2, 2009.

137. 1958 Educational Survey of the Berry Schools, 164, 168.

138. 1958 Reports of Consultants to the President, 2, Bertrand Papers, Berry College Archives.

139. Ibid., 7.

140. Ibid., 3.

141. Ibid., 8–10.

142. *Southern Highlander*, Fall 1956, 12–13.

143. Ron Pierce interview by author, October 1, 2009.

144. Gene Price interview by author, October 1, 2009.

145. Ibid.

146. Ibid.

147. Don Collins interview by author, September 12, 2009.

148. Tom Butler interview by author, September 12, 2009.

149. John Shahan interview by author, September 12, 2009.

150. Report on Initiation Activities of Varsity Club at Berry Academy, Bertrand Papers, Berry College Archives; Tom Butler interview.

151. Tom Butler interview.

152. Ibid.

153. Ibid.

154. Don Collins interview.

155. John Shahan interview.

156. Tom Butler interview.

157. Jerry Shelton interview by Ouida Dickey, June 4, 2009.

158. Fred Loveday to John Bertrand, May 7, 1965, Bertrand Papers, Berry College Archives.

CHAPTER 6

159. John R. Bertrand to Frank Leake, December 28, 1962, Bertrand Papers, Berry College Archives.

160. John Permenter, "Preliminary Survey Report on the Mount Berry School for Boys," May 31, 1963, 5, Bertrand Papers, Berry College Archives.

161. Ibid., 7.

162. Ibid., 6.

163. Ibid., 7.

164. Ibid., 8–9.

165. Ibid., 12.

166. Ibid., 13.

167. Ibid., 14.

168. Ibid., 15.

169. Ibid.

170. Ibid., 18.

171. Ibid., 19.

172. Ibid., 20.

173. Ibid., 22.

174. Ibid., 23–24.

175. John R. Bertrand to Fred H. Loveday, July 17, 1963, Bertrand Papers, Berry College Archives.

176. Thomas Gandy, "Notes on Preliminary Survey Report," Bertrand Papers, Berry College Archives.

177. Minutes of the Executive Committee of the Board of Trustees, September 16, 1963, Berry College Archives.

178. Minutes of the Board of Trustees, February 8, 1964, Berry College Archives.

179. "The Development Program at Berry," November 22, 1963, Bertrand Papers, Berry College Archives.

180. Fred Loveday to John R. Bertrand, May 31, 1963, Bertrand Papers, Berry College Archives.

181. Compilation of Information about Cases of Frank Rockwell III and Milledge Bell, June 22, 1963, Bertrand Papers, Berry College Archives.

182. Mrs. Joe Mansell to John R. Bertrand, November 22, 1963, Bertrand Papers, Berry College Archives.

183. John R. Bertrand to Mrs. Joe Mansell, November 26, 1963, Bertrand Papers, Berry College Archives.

184. "Statement presented in Hill Dining Hall at Berry Academy," December 14, 1963, Bertrand Papers, Berry College Archives.
185. "Berry Academy 1963–64 Improvements and Significant Accomplishments," Bertrand Papers, Berry College Archives.
186. Larry Campbell to John R. Bertrand, November 19, 1965, Bertrand Papers, Berry College Archives.
187. Ibid.
188. John C. Boggs, "A Statement to the President Following a Visit to Berry Academy, December 4–9, 1965, Bertrand Papers, Berry College Archives.
189. Ibid.
190. Ibid.
191. Ibid.
192. Thomas Gandy to John Bertrand, December 15, 1965, Bertrand Papers, Berry College Archives.
193. John Lipscomb, Comments on the Academy, December 22, 1965, Bertrand Papers, Berry College Archives.
194. John Lipscomb to John Bertrand, February 11, 1966, Bertrand Papers, Berry College Archives.
195. "The Situation at Berry Academy: A Review Prepared by John R. Bertrand, President," March 31, 1966, Bertrand Papers, Berry College Archives.
196. Ibid.
197. Ibid.
198. Ibid.
199. Fred Loveday to Grady Hamrick, May 2, 1966, Bertrand Papers, Berry College Archives.
200. Ibid.
201. Summary of Responses by Berry Academy Seniors to Questionnaire Administered by President John R. Bertrand on June 3, 1966, Bertrand Papers, Berry College Archives.

Chapter 7

202. John Shahan interview.
203. Robert Williams interview by Ouida W. Dickey, June 4, 2009.
204. Ibid.
205. Ibid.
206. Tom Butler interview.

207. Ibid.

208. Don Collins interview.

209. Luis Leon, telephone interview by author, May 24, 2013.

210. Ibid.

211. Ibid.

CHAPTER 8

212. Robert Crawford, Comments and Reflections About Berry Academy, September 12, 1966.

213. Frank Campbell to John Bertrand, November 2, 1966, Bertrand Papers, Berry College Archives.

214. Ibid.

215. Frank Campbell to John Bertrand, December 7, 1966, Bertrand Papers, Berry College Archives.

216. Ibid.

217. Frank Campbell, Annual Report to the President, August 2, 1967, Bertrand Papers, Berry College Archives.

218. Report by Frank Campbell to the Board of Trustees, June 24, 1967, Bertrand Papers, Berry College Archives.

219. Tom Dabney to Frank Campbell, January 5, 1968, Bertrand Papers, Berry College Archives.

220. Frank Campbell to Tom Dabney, January 5, 1968, Bertrand Papers, Berry College Archives.

221. George Faila to Frank Campbell, January 18, 1968, Bertrand Papers, Berry College Archives.

222. Jack Pigott to Frank Campbell, May 1, 1968, Bertrand Papers, Berry College Archives.

223. Jack Pigott to Frank Campbell, May 10, 1968, Bertrand Papers, Berry College Archives.

224. Jack Pigott to John Bertrand, May 22, 1968, Bertrand Papers, Berry College Archives.

225. James Leppard III to Frank Campbell, May 23, 1968, Bertrand Papers, Berry College Archives.

226. Meeting with Berry Academy Students, Faculty and Administrators, February 17, 1970, Bertrand Papers, Berry College Archives.

227. William Moss to Lamar Westcott, May 3, 1968, Bertrand Papers, Berry College Archives.

228. John Bertrand to Frank Campbell et al, November 11, 1969, Bertrand Papers, Berry College Archives.

229. John R. Lipscomb and Frank Campbell to John Bertrand, April 1, 1970, Bertrand Papers, Berry College Archives.

230. *Lavender Blue*, "Berry Meets Age of Aquarius," November 1970, 3–4.

231. John Lipscomb to John Bertrand, February 27, 1970, Bertrand Papers, Berry College Archives.

232. *Lavender Blue*, "Black Students Share Fears, Aspirations," February 1971, 6.

233. Ibid.

234. Richard Ingram to John Bertrand, January 6, 1971, Bertrand Papers, Berry College Archives.

235. Frank Campbell to John Bertrand, January 6, 1971, Bertrand Papers, Berry College Archives.

236. John Bertrand to John Permenter, September 18, 1971, Bertrand Papers, Berry College Archives.

237. Richard Ingram, "Policy Changes," December 22, 1971, Bertrand Papers, Berry College Archives.

238. Frank Campbell to John Bertrand, January 8, 1971, Bertrand Papers, Berry College Archives.

239. Ibid.

240. Dickey and Mathis, *Berry College*, 146.

241. *Rome News-Tribune*, "Berry Academy to Admit Girls for First Time," August 15, 1971, 1.

242. *Lavender Blue*, "Welcome Back, Gentlemen, and Hello Ladies!" October 1971, 3.

243. Milton McDonald to Richard Ingram, January 13, 1972, Bertrand Papers, Berry College Archives.

244. Excerpts from the meeting of the Executive Committee of the Berry Schools Board of Trustees on February 25, 1972, Bertrand Papers, Berry College Archives.

245. Tom Spector, ed., "1973 Berry Academy Yearbook," *Torch*, 7.

246. Ibid., 9.

247. *Rome News-Tribune*, "Berry Announces addition of a Middle School," April 16, 1972, 5B.

248. Spector, "1973 Yearbook," 104.

249. *Newsweek*, "Can Prep Schools Survive?," January 31, 1972, 45.

Chapter 9

250. Personal Appearance Committee Meeting, April 19, 1972, Bertrand Papers, Berry College Archives.

251. Roark Summerford interview by author, September 12, 2009.

252. Richard Ingram to All Students, Parents, and Faculty, Berry Academy, November 27, 1978, Bertrand Papers, Berry College Archives.

253. John Shahan interview.

254. Notes on meeting of January 30, 1974, Bertrand Papers, Berry College Archives.

255. *Lavender Blue*, "New Vintages on the Vine," November 1974, 3–4.

256. Milton Chambers interview by author, June 3, 2009.

257. Chuck Johnston to John Bertrand, July 7, 1978, Bertrand Papers, Berry College Archives.

258. Milton Chambers interview.

259. Memorandum to the Committee of Overseers for Berry Academy, September 19, 1978, Bertrand Papers, Berry College Archives.

260. *Rome News-Tribune*, "Berry Academy Serves...," March 2, 1976, 2; "Berry Academy Offers Unique Environment," August 1, 1976, 3B.

261. *Rome News-Tribune*, "Middle School Construction Continues," July 15, 1977, 3.

262. Tom Fraker interview by author, July 16, 2010.

263. Mary Siceloff interview by author, September 30, 2011.

264. *Rome News-Tribune*, "Scheel Appointed Berry Headmaster," June 16, 1980, 1.

265. Dan Tuck, "A Talk with the Headmaster," *Lavender Blue*, January 1981, 9.

266. William Scheel telephone interview by author, June 14, 2012.

267. Board of Trustees Minutes, October 18, 1980.

268. Academy Committee of Overseers Minutes, October 8, 1980.

269. Board of Trustees Minutes, October 17, 1981.

270. Ibid.

271. Academy Committee of Overseers Minutes, February 10, 1982.

272. Mount Berry School for Boys and Berry Academy Enrollment, 1960–1982, Executive Committee Meeting Minutes, September 22, 1982.

273. James D. Maddox to Gloria Shatto, May 25, 1982.

274. Minutes of the Executive Committee of the Board of Trustees, May 25, 1982.

275. William Scheel interview. Cecil B. Wright to H. Inman Allen, January 11, 1983.

276. Executive Committee Meeting Minutes, September 22, 1982.

277. Academy Committee of Overseers Meeting Minutes, September 29, 1982.

278. Ibid.

279. Cecil B. Wright to H. Inman Allen, January 11, 1983.

280. Board of Trustees Minutes, October 16, 1982.

281. William Scheel interview.

282. *Rome News-Tribune*, "Berry to Cease Operations at Academy," December 14, 1982, 1.

283. William Bowdoin to Berry Academy Parents, Students, Faculty and Staff and All Berry Alumni, December 13, 1982.

284. Percy Marchman to the Berry Alumni, December 13, 1982.

285. Fred Loveday to Gloria Shatto, January 13, 1983.

286. Report from the Berry Academy Parents Club, Shatto papers, Berry College Archives.

287. Stacy Robinson, "Parents Await Trustees' Decision after Meeting," *Campus Carrier*, January 27, 1983, 1.

288. Leon Lee and Stacy Robinson, "Academy Closing, Student Aid Discussed as Topics at Forum," *Campus Carrier*, February 3, 1983, 1.

289. Robinson, "Parents Await."

290. Stacy Robinson, "Law Suit Filed Against College," *Campus Carrier*, February 24, 1983, 3.

291. *Rome News-Tribune*, "Berry Faces another $20 Million Complaint," October 3, 1984.

292. Roark Summerford interview.

293. John Shahan interview.

294. Cecil B. Wright to Inman Allen.

295. David Royal, "Berry Academy: The Ending of an Era," *Rome News-Tribune*, June 5, 1983, 1B.

296. William Scheel interview.

297. Berry College Quick Facts, http://www.berry.edu/quickfacts (accessed June 9, 2012).

Epilogue

298. P.K. Boo, "Plan Unveiled; Academy to Become Lavish Nudist Resort," *Carrion*, special April Fools edition, 1983, 1.

299. Stacy Robinson, "Officials Discuss Academy's Future Use," *Campus Carrier*, April 14, 1983, 1.

300. Board of Trustees Minutes, February 18, 1983.

301. *Rome News-Tribune*, "Closed Academy Buildings at Berry Drawing Visitors, Officials Tell Judge," July 10, 1983, 1.

302. Comments to the Board of Trustees by President Gloria Shatto, October 15, 1983.

303. Deidre Mercer, "Budget Balanced," *Campus Carrier*, October 5, 1984, 1.

304. Bob Skelton interview by author, March 4, 2011.

305. S. Truett Cathy biography, http://www.truettcathy.com/about_bio.asp (accessed June 10, 2012).

306. Dickey and Mathis, *Berry College*, 172.

307. John Shahan interview.

308. Luke Lamb interview by author, March 25, 2010.

309. Stewart Fuqua interview by author June 3, 2009.

310. Leslie Almand, conversation with the author, Rome, Georgia, October 6, 2007.

Selected Bibliography

Berry College Archives, Memorial Library, Berry College

Archival Materials

RG1: Martha Berry Collection
RG4: Office of the President
   John R. Bertrand Papers
   Gloria M. Shatto Papers
RG8: Board of Trustees
   Berry Charters
   Executive Committee Meetings
   Minutes
   Reports

Periodicals

Berry Alumni Quarterly
Berry News, 1921–1924
Berry School Catalog, 1908–1909

Berry Schools Bulletin, 1910–1963
Boys Industrial School Advance, 1904–1906
Boys Industrial School Catalog, 1902–1908
Campus Carrier, 1960–1983
Lavender Blue, 1970–1983
Mount Berry News, 1924–1960
Southern Highlander, 1907–1966
The Torch, 1950–1983

OTHER SOURCES

Byers, Tracy. *For the Glory of Young Manhood and Womanhood—Yesterday, Today and Tomorrow*. 2 vols. Mount Berry, GA: Berry Schools, 1963–64.

———. *Martha Berry, the Sunday Lady of Possum Trot*. New York: Putnam's, 1932.

———. *Martha Berry's Living Glory*. Mount Berry, GA: Berry College, 1967.

Chirhart, Ann Short, and Betty Wood, eds. *Georgia Women: Their Lives and Times*. Vol.1. Athens: University of Georgia Press, 2009.

Coleman, Kenneth, ed. *History of Georgia*. Athens: University of Georgia Press, 1991.

Cook, S.H. *Half Century at Berry*. Mount Berry, GA: Berry College, 1961.

Dickey, Ouida Word. *One Hundred Years of Service: The Berry Alumni Association, 1908–2008*. Mount Berry, GA: Berry College, 2008.

Dickey, Ouida Word, and Doyle Mathis. *Berry College: A History*. Athens: University of Georgia Press, 2005.

Dickey, Ouida Word, and Herman Higgins, eds. *Berry Trails: An Historic and Contemporary Guide to Berry College*. Centennial ed. Mount Berry, GA: Berry College, 2001.

Kane, Harnett, and Inez Henry. *Miracle in the Mountains*. Garden City, NY: Doubleday, 1956.

Mathis, Doyle, and Ouida Dickey, eds. *Martha Berry: Sketches of Her Schools and College*. Atlanta, GA: Wings, 2001.

Pendley, Evelyn Hoge. *Education for Service: The Berry Schools, 1902–1979*. Mount Berry, GA: Berry College, 1985.

———. *A Lady I Loved*. Mount Berry, GA: Berry College, 1966.

———. *Sixty Years of Education for Service: An Account of the Administrations of Berry College and the Mount Berry School for Boys*. Mount Berry, GA: Berry College, 1963.

INDEX

About the Author

J ennifer Dickey is a graduate of Berry Academy and Berry College and the former director and curator of Oak Hill and the Martha Berry Museum. She is currently an assistant professor and coordinator of the Public History Program at Kennesaw State University. Dr. Dickey has a master's degree in international business from the University of South Carolina and a master's degree in heritage preservation and a PhD in public history from Georgia State University.